BRIDGING THE GAP

STRENGTHENING SCHOOL-COMMUNITY PARTNERSHIPS THROUGH CULTURAL BROKERS

DR. OSCAR HARRIS

DISCLAIMER

The information provided in this book is designed to provide helpful information on the subjects discussed. This book is not intended to be used, and should not be used, as a sole source of information for making educational, legal, or any other professional decisions.

The views expressed in this book are those of the author(s) and do not necessarily reflect the views of the publisher. The publisher and author are not responsible for any specific educational or community outcomes that result from the application of the information provided in this book.

While examples of school-community partnerships and roles of cultural brokers are drawn from research and real-life scenarios, they should be seen as illustrative and not prescriptive. Every educational setting and community is unique, and strategies should be adapted to fit specific contexts and needs.

TABLE OF CONTENTS

CHAPTER 1

Schools are much more than places where books are opened, lessons are taught, and exams are taken. They are vibrant learning centers where the future is shaped through textbooks, real-life experiences, and community engagement. The importance of forming strong partnerships between schools and their communities cannot be understated, as these relationships play a crucial role in enhancing students' educational journey.

Imagine a school focusing on academic achievements and nurturing its students by connecting them with the broader community. This is where the nexus of school-community partnerships comes into play. These partnerships open opportunities for students to learn beyond the conventional classroom setting. They provide students the chance to work on actual issues, put their knowledge to use in real-world situations, and acquire skills that will be vital to their futures, both personally and professionally.

One of the most significant benefits of school-community partnerships is the rich resource pool available to schools. Local businesses, cultural organizations, and service groups often possess knowledge, skills, and experiences. When these entities collaborate with schools, they can offer students unique learning experiences, internships, and volunteer opportunities that enrich their understanding and prepare them for the complexities of adult life.

Moreover, when communities and schools come together, they create a supportive network that promotes students' well-being. This support goes beyond academic learning; it encompasses emotional and social support, making students feel valued and part of a larger community. Such a nurturing environment is crucial for developing confident, well-rounded individuals ready to face the world's challenges.

However, building and maintaining these partnerships is sometimes a difficult walk in the park. It requires effort, understanding, and a shared vision from schools and community members. Communication is key. To obtain mutual advantages, both parties must be transparent about their expectations, aims, and plans to collaborate. This partnership might result in innovative educational initiatives that address students' many requirements and increase the relevance and engagement of learning.

Furthermore, these partnerships can also address and bridge societal gaps. Schools serve students from diverse backgrounds with unique cultural, social, and economic contexts. Community partnerships can play a pivotal role in ensuring that all students have access to the same opportunities, irrespective of their backgrounds. Schools can offer a more inclusive education that respects and celebrates diversity through such collaborations.

The impact of school-community partnerships extends beyond the immediate educational benefits. They foster a sense of belonging and community spirit among students, parents, teachers, and community members. This collective effort enhances the quality of education and strengthens the community. It's about building an ecosystem of support where all members benefit from and contribute to each other's success.

The essence of school-community partnerships lies in the mutual belief that education is a shared responsibility. It's not just the job of schools to educate today's young minds; it's a collective mission that involves the whole community. When schools open their doors to community involvement and when communities embrace the role of co-educators, the educational experience becomes richer, more meaningful, and better aligned with the real world.

The significance of school-community partnerships in the educational landscape cannot be overstated. They are instrumental in providing students with a holistic education that prepares them for the future. Schools can offer more dynamic, relevant, and engaging learning experiences by fostering these partnerships. It's about taking the journey together, where schools and communities work hand in hand to support the growth and development of students. This collaborative approach enriches the educational experience and builds more robust, resilient communities.

Introduction to the concept of cultural brokers

In the rich tapestry of modern society, schools and communities are vibrant hubs of diverse cultures and backgrounds. Amidst this diversity, there exists a need for a special kind of bridge to connect these different worlds for the betterment of education. This is where the concept of cultural brokers comes into the picture. Cultural brokers are not just individuals but the essence of understanding, empathy, and connection in the educational landscape. Their role is to ensure that the school and its community co-exist and is deeply intertwined, benefiting from each other's richness and diversity.

Cultural brokers possess unique skills and insights that enable them to navigate the complexities of different cultural backgrounds. They understand the nuances of various cultures represented in the community and can communicate effectively across these cultural divides. Because of this capacity, cultural brokers are crucial in fostering a learning atmosphere where each student feels heard, recognized, and respected. They work tirelessly to ensure that the educational content and methods are inclusive and reflect the community's diverse perspectives.

Moreover, cultural brokers advocate for students and families who might feel marginalized or misunderstood within the school system. They are the voice for those needing more support to speak up, ensuring their needs and concerns are addressed. Cultural brokers help build trust between the school and the community by doing so. This trust is crucial for creating a supportive educational environment where students thrive.

Cultural brokers' role extends beyond addressing cultural differences. They also play a critical part in identifying and leveraging the unique strengths and resources each culture brings to the educational table. Whether it's introducing new perspectives in the curriculum, organizing community-led workshops, or facilitating cultural exchange programs, cultural brokers work to enrich the academic experience for all students. This enhances the learning journey and prepares students to navigate a globalized world with understanding and respect for diverse cultures.

Cultural brokers also serve as mentors and role models for students, showing them the power of cultural diversity and the importance of bridging cultural gaps. They inspire students to embrace their cultural identities while being open to learning about and respecting others. This fosters a school environment where diversity is not just tolerated but celebrated.

The impact of cultural brokers on school-community partnerships cannot be overstated. They are critical in transforming these partnerships into dynamic, collaborative efforts that benefit everyone involved. Through their work, cultural brokers help schools and communities move beyond simple cooperation to a deeper level of engagement. They ensure that community resources are effectively integrated into the educational process, making learning more relevant and accessible to students from all backgrounds.

However, becoming a successful cultural broker requires more than a deep understanding of different cultures. It requires patience, empathy, and relentlessly fostering positive change. Cultural brokers often navigate complex, sensitive situations, requiring a delicate balance between advocating for change and respecting the traditions and values of different cultural groups. It's a challenging role that is essential for creating inclusive, supportive educational environments.

In essence, cultural brokers are the heart and soul of the efforts to bridge the gap between schools and the diverse communities they serve. Their work is fundamental in building educational environments where every student, regardless of their cultural background, has the opportunity to succeed and flourish. By promoting understanding, respect, and collaboration, cultural brokers enhance the educational experience and contribute to a more inclusive, empathetic society.

As society continues to become more diverse, the role of cultural brokers in education will only grow in importance. Their work fostering understanding and connection between different cultural groups is essential in preparing students to thrive in a multicultural world. Cultural brokers remind us that our differences are not barriers but opportunities for enrichment, learning, and growth. Their efforts paved the way for a future where diversity is celebrated and education is genuinely inclusive.

Dr. Oscar Harris's study on Epstein's framework

Dr. Oscar Harris's work highlights an essential aspect of education beyond the usual focus on subjects and grades. His study dives into the depths of Epstein's framework, a model that advocates for the active involvement of teachers, students, families, and the broader community in the educational process. This framework isn't just a theory; it's a call to action for a more collaborative and inclusive approach to education. Through his research, Dr. Harris provides us with a closer look at how this model can be applied in real life, transforming how we think about and engage with education.

Epstein's framework outlines six types of involvement: communicating, decision-making, learning at home, volunteering, parenting, and collaborating with the community (Epstein et al., 2019). Each type is a pillar for building a solid educational structure that holistically supports students' learning and development. Dr. Harris's study delves into each of these areas, exploring their impact and how they can be effectively implemented to enhance the educational experience for students.

One of the key insights from Dr. Harris's research is the importance of creating a welcoming environment for all families. He emphasizes that schools need to reach out and engage parents and guardians in meaningful ways, making them feel valued and part of their children's learning journey. This involves clear and open communication, offering various opportunities for involvement, and recognizing the unique contributions that each family can bring to the educational community.

Dr. Harris also highlights the role of volunteering in bringing the community into the school. By opening their doors to the community, schools may access a multitude of resources, expertise, and information that can enhance the educational experience. Volunteers can help instructors, mentor students, and provide extracurricular activities to create a lively and dynamic learning environment.

Learning at home is another critical area explored in Dr. Harris's study. He advocates for schools to support parents in creating a conducive learning environment at home, offering resources and guidance on effectively engaging with their children's education. This partnership between schools and families can significantly impact students' academic success and attitudes toward learning.

Dr. Harris's research also emphasizes decision-making and collaboration with the community. He makes the case for a more democratic approach to education, one in which community members and families are involved in determining the laws, policies, and procedures that impact the education of their children. This collaborative effort can lead to more responsive and effective educational programs that meet students' diverse needs.

Dr. Harris's work underscores the practical application of Epstein's framework in fostering a collaborative, inclusive, and holistic approach to education. His research is not just about theories and concepts; it's about bringing those ideas to life in ways that make a real difference for students, families, and communities. Dr. Harris shows us through his study that when schools, families, and communities work together, they can create a powerful support system that enhances students' learning and development.

Moreover, Dr. Harris's results should serve as a roadmap for educators and educational institutions attempting to bridge the gap between their organizations and their communities. It offers a roadmap for building more robust, more meaningful partnerships that can transform the academic landscape. Dr. Harris provides valuable insights and strategies for engaging all stakeholders in the educational process by focusing on the practical implementation of Epstein's framework.

One of the most compelling aspects of Dr. Harris's study is the real-world examples he provides, illustrating how schools have successfully applied Epstein's framework to improve student outcomes. These case studies inspire and prove that with commitment and collaboration, schools can create a more inclusive, engaging, and effective educational environment.

In addition, Dr. Harris's research illuminates the challenges schools may face in implementing Epstein's framework and offers solutions to overcome these obstacles. He acknowledges that change can be challenging. Nevertheless, schools may overcome these obstacles and advance toward a more inclusive and collaborative educational model with tenacity and a common goal.

In essence, Dr. Oscar Harris's study on Epstein's framework offers a fresh perspective on the critical role that families and communities play in education. It challenges traditional notions of schooling and calls for a more integrated approach that recognizes the interconnectedness of schools, families, and communities. Through his research, Dr. Harris contributes to the academic discourse on educational partnerships and provides a practical guide for schools looking to enhance their engagement with families and the wider community. His work is a testament to the power of collaboration and its positive impact on student's education and their lives beyond the classroom.

Purpose and scope of the book

This book embarks on a journey to explore the dynamic interplay between schools and communities and the pivotal role of cultural brokers in knitting these two worlds together. The educational landscape is ever-evolving, marked by diversity and complexity. In this context, the traditional boundaries of schooling are expanding, calling for a more integrated approach that brings together various stakeholders in the educational process. This book aims to illuminate the pathways through which school-community partnerships can be strengthened, leveraging the unique position of cultural brokers to foster collaboration, understanding, and mutual respect.

At its core, this book aims to serve as a comprehensive guide for educators, community leaders, policymakers, and anyone interested in the educational well-being of students. It seeks to answer essential concerns like the best ways for communities and schools to collaborate, the function of cultural intermediaries in fostering these relationships, and doable tactics for boosting involvement and teamwork. This book aims to offer readers a thorough grasp of the significance of school-community collaborations and the transformational potential of cultural brokerage through theoretical ideas, real-world examples, and expert analysis.

The scope of the book is broad yet focused. It covers various aspects of school-community partnerships, from their definition and significance to the benefits and challenges they present. It delves into the historical context and current state of these partnerships, providing a comprehensive background against which the role of cultural brokers is examined. The book further explores the concept of cultural brokers, their definitions, and the skills and characteristics that make them effective. Through case studies and analysis, the book illustrates how cultural brokers can successfully facilitate partnership building, highlighting the practical application of their work in diverse educational settings.

Moreover, the book examines the findings of Dr. Oscar Harris's study on Epstein's framework, drawing out the implications for school-community partnerships. It uses this research to showcase the effectiveness of structured partnership models and their impact on student achievement and community well-being. Strategies for enhancing partnerships through cultural brokers are discussed, offering readers a toolkit of approaches for establishing communication channels, building trust, and leveraging community assets.

The challenges and barriers to successful partnership development are not overlooked. The book addresses the common obstacles encountered in this work, including cultural, linguistic, and systemic barriers. It provides strategies for navigating these challenges and offers insights into how power dynamics and conflicts can be managed and resolved. Success stories and case studies are included to inspire and guide readers in their efforts to overcome these hurdles.

In addition to addressing the current state of school-community partnerships, the book explores future directions and innovations. It discusses emerging trends, the potential for leveraging technology, and new models of cultural brokerage.

Recommendations for policymakers, educators, and community leaders are provided to spur action and innovation in developing more inclusive, effective, and sustainable partnerships. The book's conclusion combines the key insights and lessons learned, offering a call to action to strengthen school-community partnerships. It highlights how critical cultural intermediaries are to encouraging teamwork and improving students' educational experiences. The book closes by exploring school-community partnerships, underscoring the importance of continued learning, adaptation, and commitment to this vital work.

In essence, this book is about building bridges between schools and their communities, between theory and practice, and between diverse groups of people. It celebrates the power of collaboration and the belief that together, we can create educational environments where every student has the opportunity to thrive. This book invites readers to embark on this journey of discovery and transformation, armed with knowledge, strategies, and a vision for a more connected, inclusive, and vibrant educational future.

CHAPTER 2

Understanding the definition and significance of school-community partnerships is like peeling back the layers of an onion. Each layer reveals a deeper understanding of how these partnerships can transform the educational landscape, creating environments where students can thrive academically and as well-rounded individuals.

School-community partnerships are collaborative relationships between educational institutions and their broader communities. These partnerships are built on the premise that schools are not isolated entities but integral parts of their communities. They involve many participants, including families, local businesses, social service agencies, and cultural organizations. The goal is to harness these groups' collective resources and strengths to support student learning, well-being, and the development of a vibrant community life.

The significance of these partnerships cannot be overstated. In an educational context, the benefits extend far beyond the classroom walls. For students, these partnerships provide opportunities for real-world learning experiences that can enhance their academic achievement and personal growth. They offer chances to connect with mentors, engage in service projects, and gain exposure to career paths and cultural experiences they might not otherwise encounter. This all-encompassing approach to education builds resilience and an optimistic attitude toward the future by giving children a feeling of purpose and belonging.

For teachers and schools, community partnerships can lead to a more enriched curriculum and access to additional resources, including volunteers, funding, and materials. This support can alleviate some of the pressures on schools to meet the diverse needs of their students on their own. It also opens doors to innovative teaching methods and learning experiences that reflect the community's unique culture and assets.

Communities also benefit significantly from these partnerships. Schools can become hubs of community life, where families feel welcomed and valued, and community members come together to support the next generation. This can lead to stronger community ties, improved public spaces, and greater civic responsibility among students and residents. Furthermore, these partnerships can address community issues directly, creating solutions informed by those who live and work in the community.

The significance of school-community partnerships also lies in their ability to level the playing field for all students, especially those from marginalized or underserved backgrounds. By drawing on community resources, schools can offer support and opportunities that may be lacking in students' homes or neighborhoods. These include social and health assistance, after-school activities, educational resources, and technology access. Such support is crucial in breaking down barriers to student success and promoting equity and inclusion within the educational system.

Moreover, these partnerships offer a powerful antidote to the isolation and disconnection that can plague modern society. They remind us that education is a shared responsibility that benefits from the involvement and investment of the entire community. In this way, school-community partnerships can serve as a model for building more robust, more cohesive societies.

In building these partnerships, schools, and communities embark on a journey of mutual discovery. Schools learn more about their students' and their families' needs, strengths, and cultures. Community members also better comprehend the potential and problems found in the educational system. This mutual understanding is the foundation for effective collaboration and positive change.

However, creating and sustaining these alliances requires considerable work, adaptability, and readiness to share knowledge and insights. It involves navigating differences in culture, perspective, and priorities, finding common ground, and working towards shared goals. The most successful partnerships are those built on trust, respect, and a commitment to open communication and ongoing dialogue.

The concept and importance of school-community partnerships emphasize how they may improve education, build stronger communities, and provide all parties involved with a feeling of purpose and belonging. These partnerships represent a powerful strategy for preparing students to succeed in school and life. Our challenges and possibilities will be growing these partnerships and ensuring they are inclusive, egalitarian, and adaptable enough to satisfy the shifting demands of communities and students. In doing so, we can create educational environments that not only support academic achievement but also promote the well-being and development of all students as engaged, compassionate citizens of the world.

Benefits and challenges

Embarking on the journey of school-community partnerships brings many benefits, though it still has its fair share of challenges. These partnerships are akin to a collaborative dance where every step forward can sometimes be met with a stumble, yet the overall performance has the potential to captivate and inspire.

The benefits of these partnerships are profound and multifaceted. They create enriched learning environments that extend beyond the traditional classroom setting. Students gain access to a broader array of educational resources and experiences, from local experts sharing their knowledge to community sites becoming living classrooms. This real-world connection makes learning more engaging and helps students see the relevance of their studies in their daily lives and future careers.

Moreover, these partnerships often lead to improved academic outcomes. With the community investing in their success, students receive the encouragement and support needed to excel. Tutoring, mentoring, and after-school programs provided by community partners can significantly impact students' academic performance, particularly those who may need extra help.

Students' social and emotional development is also significantly boosted. Students learn valuable life skills through interaction with diverse community members, such as communication, empathy, and teamwork. They develop a sense of belonging and responsibility towards their community, which can foster self-esteem and a positive attitude towards learning.

The benefits for the community are equally impactful. Schools develop into thriving hubs of community life where families and neighbors are made to feel important and welcomed. These partnerships can rejuvenate community spirit and pride, leading to more robust, cohesive neighborhoods. Moreover, by addressing community needs directly, such as literacy programs or health services, schools can play a central role in improving the overall well-being of the area they serve.

However, establishing and nurturing these partnerships has its challenges. One of the most significant hurdles is the difference in culture and communication styles between educational institutions and community organizations. Schools operate within a specific set of policies and procedures, which can sometimes clash with community groups' more flexible, informal approach. Bridging this gap requires patience, understanding, and a willingness to adapt from both sides.

Resource constraints can also pose a challenge. Effective partnerships require time, effort, and sometimes financial investment. In an era where schools and community organizations often face tight budgets, finding the resources to support these collaborations can take time and effort. It calls for innovative thinking and a dedication to seeing collaboration as an essential investment in the community's and kids' futures.

Moreover, building trust and mutual respect takes time. Faith is the cornerstone of a successful connection, and faith must be gained via regular, honest communication and similar experiences. Misunderstandings and setbacks can occur, especially in the early stages of partnership development, which can test the commitment of both parties to the collaboration.

The challenge of ensuring equity and inclusion within partnerships must be addressed. These partnerships must benefit all students, including those from marginalized or underserved communities. This requires a deliberate focus on equity, ensuring that the programs and opportunities created through partnerships are accessible to every student, regardless of their background.

Despite these challenges, the journey towards effective school-community partnerships is worth the effort. The key to overcoming obstacles lies in maintaining a clear focus on the shared goal: enhancing the educational experience and outcomes for students while contributing to the health and vitality of the community. It involves a commitment to ongoing dialogue, flexibility, and a willingness to learn from each other.

In navigating the complexities of these partnerships, it's important to celebrate small victories and learn from setbacks. Each step forward, each successful collaboration, and each challenge overcome brings valuable lessons that can strengthen the partnership and deepen the impact on students and the community.

The benefits of school-community partnerships are clear. They offer a powerful means to enhance education, foster student development, and strengthen communities. While the challenges are real, they are not insurmountable. With commitment, creativity, and collaboration, schools and communities can work together to create partnerships that are not only effective but truly transformative. Though filled with hurdles, this journey promises a brighter future for students and communities, making it a path worth pursuing.

Historical context and evolution

The story of school-community partnerships is one of growth and evolution, shaped by societies and the education system's changing needs. These partnerships have only sometimes been a formal part of educational planning. Still, their roots run deep into history, reflecting a long-standing recognition of the value of community involvement in education.

In the early days, the concept of schooling was inherently community-based. One-room schoolhouses served as the heart of small towns, where the lines between the school and the community were naturally blurred. Teachers were integral community members, and parents and local citizens were actively involved in the educational process. This close-knit relationship ensured that the curriculum was directly relevant to the community's needs, and everyone played a part in supporting the academic development of children.

The connection between schools and communities diminished as societies became more complex and urbanized. The introduction of formal education systems and the growth of cities created a more structured approach to schooling, which, while expanding access to education, often led to a separation between schools and their communities. The Industrial Revolution further widened this gap as schools became focused on preparing students for the workforce, adhering to standardized curricula that left little room for community involvement.

However, the 20th century witnessed a growing awareness of the limitations of an education system isolated from its community. Educators and reformers began to argue for a more holistic approach to education that recognized the importance of students' social, emotional, and physical well-being alongside academic achievement. This period saw the emergence of progressive education movements that advocated for experiential learning, community service, and the integration of life skills into the curriculum.

The civil rights movement and the fight for educational equity further highlighted the importance of schools interacting with their communities. It became clear that addressing the complex challenges facing students, especially those from marginalized and underserved communities, required a concerted effort that combined the resources and strengths of schools with those of families, local organizations, and businesses.

In response to these evolving understandings, the late 20th and early 21st centuries have deliberately moved towards re-establishing and strengthening school-community partnerships. Educational policies and initiatives began to emphasize the importance of family and community engagement in supporting student success. Recognizing that learning occurs in classrooms and within the broader context of students' lives has led to innovative partnership models that seek to bridge the gap between schools and communities.

These models vary widely, reflecting different communities' diverse needs and resources. Some focus on bringing community resources into schools, such as health and social services, to address barriers to learning. Others emphasize extending the classroom into the community through service learning projects, internships, and partnerships with local businesses and organizations. Technology has dramatically aided this progress, which provides new avenues for cooperation and communication between communities and schools through online platforms and virtual learning possibilities.

Despite the challenges, the evolution of school-community partnerships reflects a growing consensus on the value of these collaborations. Research and experience have shown that when schools and communities work together, students benefit from a richer, more relevant education that prepares them for the complexities of the modern world. Communities also thrive as schools become centers of civic life and engagement, fostering a sense of shared responsibility and collective well-being.

Today, the journey continues. As we face new challenges, from global pandemics to social and environmental issues, the importance of strong, resilient school-community partnerships is more apparent than ever. These partnerships are not just a nice-to-have addition to the education system; they are essential components of a holistic approach to learning and development. They represent a commitment to the idea that education is a shared endeavor that requires the involvement, investment, and collaboration of everyone in the community.

In this light, the historical context and evolution of school-community partnerships offer valuable lessons for the future. They remind us of the power of community in shaping the lives of young people and the importance of continually adapting and innovating to meet the needs of students and societies. As we look ahead, the story of these partnerships is still being written, with each chapter offering new opportunities to create more inclusive, effective, and vibrant educational environments for all students.

Current state of school-community partnerships

The landscape of school-community partnerships is as dynamic as it is diverse, continuously evolving to meet the changing needs of students, schools, and communities. These collaborations are more important now than ever, as they significantly impact how young people learn and how communities are structured worldwide. The current state of these collaborations reflects a rich tapestry of innovation, challenges, and opportunities, all aimed at fostering environments where students can excel academically and personally.

In recent years, there has been a marked increase in the recognition of the value communities bring to the educational equation. Schools are no longer seen as isolated entities but as integral parts of their communities, with the potential to benefit from and contribute to the community's well-being. This shift in perspective has led to a surge in efforts to forge strong, sustainable partnerships between schools and various community stakeholders, including local businesses, non-profit organizations, cultural institutions, and social service agencies.

One of the hallmarks of the current state of school-community partnerships is their diversity. These collaborations can take many forms, from mentorship programs connecting students with local professionals to partnerships with cultural organizations that enrich the curriculum with arts and cultural education. Community service projects, internships, and apprenticeship opportunities exemplify how these partnerships provide students with hands-on learning experiences that prepare them for future careers and civic engagement.

One major factor fostering creativity in school-community relationships is technology. Digital platforms facilitate communication and collaboration among schools, families, and community members, making coordinating efforts and sharing resources easier. Social media and other online tools have also opened up new avenues for community involvement in education, allowing for greater flexibility in how community members can contribute their time and expertise.

Despite the growing recognition of their importance, school-community partnerships face several challenges. One of the most pressing issues is the need for sustainable funding and resources. Collaboration depends on contributions or grant money, which needs to be revised and insufficient to pay for long-term projects. This financial uncertainty can make it difficult for schools and community organizations to plan and implement effective programs. Another challenge is the need for effective coordination and communication. Successful partnerships require a high level of coordination to align multiple stakeholders' goals, activities, and resources. This can be complex, particularly in large or diverse communities where partners may have different priorities and expectations. Additionally, ensuring that all voices are heard and valued, especially those of marginalized or underserved community members, remains a critical concern.

Despite these obstacles, several encouraging fruitful collaborations between schools and the community have significantly improved students' lives and the community's growth. These partnerships often thrive on innovation, adaptability, and a shared commitment to the common good. They demonstrate that creativity, collaboration, and a focus on equity can overcome obstacles and achieve meaningful outcomes. Looking ahead, the future of school-community partnerships holds excellent promise. There is a growing awareness of the need for holistic education that addresses students' academic, social, and emotional needs. This recognition drives efforts to create more integrated and comprehensive partnership-building approaches, focusing on inclusivity and sustainability.

To maximize their potential, school-community partnerships must continue evolving and embracing new ideas and technologies while staying grounded in mutual respect and shared responsibility. By doing this, they may support the vibrancy and resilience of communities worldwide while continuing to play a critical role in educating students about the possibilities and challenges of the twenty-first century.

In essence, the current state of school-community partnerships is characterized by a mix of enthusiasm and challenges, innovation, and the need for stability. As these partnerships continue to develop, they offer a powerful means to enhance education, nurture student development, and strengthen the social fabric of communities. The journey ahead is full of potential, inviting schools, communities, and all stakeholders to join forces and work towards a brighter, more inclusive future for education.

CHAPTER 3

In the tapestry of our diverse society, the role of cultural brokers stands out as a beacon of connection and understanding. These individuals are the architects of bridges between differing cultures, playing a pivotal role in blending the diverse hues of society into a cohesive masterpiece. To understand their significance, we must first delve into what it means to be a cultural broker and the multifaceted role they embody.

A cultural broker can be considered a translator, not just of languages. They translate cultures, values, norms, and expectations, facilitating understanding and cooperation between individuals or groups from different cultural backgrounds. This role is especially crucial in environments like schools, where the population is increasingly diverse, and the need for mutual understanding and respect is paramount.

The essence of a cultural broker's work lies in their ability to navigate the complexities of artistic identities with empathy and insight. Their profound comprehension of the cultural contexts of their communities enables them to function as efficient mediators. Their work involves more than just conveying messages; it's about interpreting the context, the unspoken nuances, and the emotional undertones of interactions. This delicate balancing act helps foster an environment of inclusivity and respect where diverse perspectives are acknowledged, valued, and integrated.

Cultural brokers are crucial in bridging the gap between schools and the diverse communities they serve. They work closely with teachers, students, and families, ensuring the educational experience is relevant and accessible to everyone, regardless of their cultural background. By doing this, individuals contribute to developing a learning environment that honors and represents the community's diversity.

Cultural brokers also advocate for students and families from culturally diverse backgrounds. They help schools understand the unique needs and strengths of their communities, advocating for policies and practices that are culturally responsive and equitable. This advocacy is crucial in addressing systemic barriers to education and ensuring that all students have the opportunity to succeed.

Moreover, cultural brokers facilitate communication and understanding between schools and families. They help to break down language and cultural barriers, ensuring that families are informed and engaged in their children's education. This engagement is vital for fostering positive relationships between schools and communities, leading to better student educational outcomes.

Cultural brokers extend beyond the walls of schools. They work within the broader community, fostering partnerships and collaborations that enrich the educational experience. This might involve connecting schools with local organizations, businesses, and cultural groups, creating meaningful opportunities for students to learn from and engage with their community.

Cultural brokers are also instrumental in promoting cultural competence among educators and students. They provide training and resources that help schools embrace diversity and incorporate multicultural perspectives into the curriculum. In today's globalized society, when empathy and cultural awareness are vital for personal and professional success, this activity is crucial in preparing students for life in the real world.

Despite their critical role, cultural brokers often face challenges in their work. These can include navigating systemic biases, overcoming language barriers, and building trust within communities that may have experienced marginalization or exclusion. However, their ability to overcome these obstacles and forge meaningful connections is a testament to their dedication and skill.

Cultural brokers are vital catalysts for change, promoting understanding, respect, and cooperation in diverse settings. Their work in educational environments is particularly impactful, helping to create inclusive communities where every student has the opportunity to thrive. As society continues to become more diverse, the role of cultural brokers will only grow in importance, making their contribution to cultural understanding and community cohesion invaluable. Through their efforts, cultural brokers enhance the educational experience and pave the way for a more inclusive and empathetic society.

Importance of cultural competence in partnership development

In today's global village, where the world is more interconnected than ever, cultural competence has emerged as a cornerstone in developing effective partnerships, especially in education and community collaboration. Cultural competency is an essential set of skills for anybody trying to create connections across disparate cultures; it is not merely a catchphrase. It is necessary to recognize its value in forming alliances as it is the foundation for the capacity to comprehend, relate to, and work well with others from diverse cultural backgrounds.

Cultural competence involves:

- Being aware of one's worldview.
- Gaining knowledge of different artistic practices and world views.
- Acquiring cross-cultural communication and interpersonal abilities.

This competence is particularly vital in educational settings and community partnerships, where the diversity of stakeholders requires an inclusive and respectful approach.

One primary reason cultural competence is crucial in partnership development is that it fosters trust. Trust is the foundation upon which collaboration is built in any partnership. When parties involved demonstrate an understanding and respect for each other's cultural backgrounds, it creates a sense of safety and openness. In this environment, everyone feels comfortable expressing their thoughts, beliefs, and cultural practices without fear of judgment or misunderstanding, creating more meaningful and profound interactions.

Moreover, cultural competence enriches partnership development by enhancing communication. Good communication is essential to any successful collaboration, but miscommunication may happen fast when cultural differences are involved. A culturally competent individual can navigate these differences, ensuring that messages are transmitted, received, and understood. This skill is essential when addressing sensitive issues or resolving conflicts that may arise within the partnership.

Additionally, cultural competence leads to more inclusive decision-making. In school-community partnerships, decisions must reflect all stakeholders' needs and perspectives. A culturally competent approach ensures that diverse viewpoints are considered and valued, leading to more equitable and effective outcomes. This inclusivity strengthens the partnership and enhances its impact on the community it serves.

Cultural competence is also critical in identifying and leveraging each culture's unique strengths and resources. Every culture has assets that can enrich educational experiences and community initiatives. By recognizing and valuing these contributions, partnerships can develop programs and strategies that are innovative, dynamic, and reflective of the community's diversity. This approach bolsters the partnership's objectives and promotes a sense of pride and ownership among all involved.

Furthermore, developing cultural competence within partnerships is essential for addressing and mitigating biases and inequities. Biases, whether conscious or unconscious, can undermine the effectiveness of partnerships, leading to disparities in access, participation, and outcomes. A commitment to cultural competence involves actively challenging these biases, ensuring that the partnership operates on principles of fairness and justice. This commitment is vital for creating alliances that genuinely benefit all community members.

However, becoming culturally competent requires ongoing learning and development rather than a one-time accomplishment. It requires ongoing education, reflection, and adaptation. Partnerships must invest in cultural competence training and development, creating opportunities for stakeholders to learn from each other and deepen their understanding of different cultural perspectives. This investment enhances the partnership's effectiveness and contributes to everyone involver's personal and professional development.

The importance of cultural competence in developing partnerships, especially within education and community collaboration, cannot be overstated. Cultural competence is the glue that holds diverse groups together, enabling them to work towards common goals with mutual respect and understanding. By fostering trust, enhancing communication, ensuring inclusivity, leveraging cultural strengths, and addressing biases, cultural competence strengthens partnerships, making them more effective and impactful. As our world grows more diverse, navigating and bridging cultural differences will remain an indispensable skill for anyone looking to make a positive difference through collaboration.

Characteristics and skills of effective cultural brokers

Navigating the complexities of diverse cultural landscapes requires unique characteristics and skills, particularly for those serving as cultural brokers. These individuals act as bridges, connecting different cultural worlds to promote understanding, cooperation, and respect. The effectiveness of cultural brokers hinges on a distinctive blend of personal attributes and professional abilities that enable them to navigate cultural differences with ease and grace.

First and foremost, empathy stands out as a cornerstone characteristic of effective cultural brokers. This deep, intuitive understanding allows them to perceive and appreciate the feelings and perspectives of individuals from diverse backgrounds. Empathy enables cultural brokers to connect on a human level, building trust and opening lines of communication that transcend cultural boundaries.

Another critical characteristic is cultural awareness. Effective cultural brokers possess a profound understanding of both their own culture and the cultures of those they serve. This awareness goes beyond surface-level differences, delving into the nuances of social norms, values, traditions, and communication styles.

With this knowledge, cultural brokers can anticipate and navigate misunderstandings with sensitivity and respect.

Adaptability is also essential. Cultural brokers often find themselves in dynamic, sometimes unpredictable environments. Despite difficulties, they can facilitate beneficial interactions and outcomes because of their capacity to adapt and respond to changing circumstances and demands.

Effective cultural brokers also exhibit excellent communication skills. They are adept at verbal and non-verbal communication and can convey and interpret messages accurately and sensitively across cultural divides. This skill set includes active listening, which entirely concentrates on what is being said rather than just passively hearing the message. Through active listening, cultural brokers can understand communication's underlying meanings and emotions, which are crucial for resolving conflicts and building deeper relationships.

Another indispensable skill is mediation. Cultural brokers often find themselves mediators in resolving conflicts or misunderstandings arising from cultural differences. They must remain neutral, understand all sides of an issue, and facilitate solutions that all parties can accept. This requires patience, creativity, and a deep commitment to fairness.

Knowledge acquisition and dissemination are other skills that set effective cultural brokers apart. They are lifelong learners, constantly seeking to expand their understanding of the cultures they work with. Moreover, they are skilled educators, able to share their knowledge with others in accessible and engaging ways. This ability to learn and teach is crucial for raising cultural awareness and competence among the groups they serve.

Effective cultural brokers are characterized by their integrity and respect for all cultures. They approach their work with a genuine desire to foster mutual understanding and respect. This integrity ensures that their efforts are driven by the best interests of the communities and individuals they serve rather than personal biases or agendas.

In practice, the work of cultural brokers is as varied as the communities and individuals they serve. It might involve facilitating community dialogues, translating documents and conversations, organizing cultural competency pieces of training, or working one-on-one with individuals to help them navigate cultural differences. Effective cultural brokers' core characteristics and skills remain the same regardless of the specific tasks.

Cultural brokers have a profound impact on the communities and organizations they serve. By bridging cultural gaps, they prevent misunderstandings and conflicts and enrich the cultural fabric of the groups they work with. Their efforts result in more peaceful, inclusive settings where diversity is cherished, and everyone is made to feel important and understood.

Cultural brokers' role is indispensable in today's increasingly diverse and interconnected world. The characteristics and skills they embody enable them to perform their complex and nuanced roles effectively. Empathy, cultural awareness, adaptability, communication, mediation, knowledge acquisition, and a deep respect for all cultures pave the way for greater understanding and cooperation among diverse groups. Their work is a testament to the power of human connection across cultural divides, highlighting the possibility of a more inclusive and empathetic society.

Case studies illustrating successful cultural brokerage

Delving into the world of cultural brokerage through the lens of case studies offers a unique opportunity to see theory in action and understand the profound impact that effective cultural mediation can have on communities and institutions alike. These real-world examples serve as beacons of success, demonstrating how cultural brokers bridge gaps, foster understanding, and cultivate enriching partnerships that benefit everyone involved.

The first case takes us to a bustling city school district that faced significant challenges in engaging its diverse student population, including many immigrant families. There were many language obstacles, cultural misinterpretations, and low faith in the school system. Enter Maria, a cultural broker with a deep understanding of the community's diverse cultural backgrounds. She initiated a series of parent engagement workshops in multiple languages, where families could learn about the educational system, express their concerns, and share their cultural values. Maria also trained school staff on cultural sensitivity and inclusive communication practices. Over time, her efforts led to increased parental involvement, improved student attendance rates, and a more inclusive school culture that celebrated diversity.

Another inspiring example comes from a healthcare initiative in a rural area with a significant Indigenous population. Historical mistrust between the Indigenous communities and healthcare providers has led to disparities in healthcare access and outcomes. Tom, a cultural broker with ties to medical and Indigenous communities, worked to bridge this divide. He organized community meetings where healthcare providers could listen to and learn from Indigenous people's experiences and perspectives. Tom facilitated culturally tailored health education programs and advocated for including traditional healing practices alongside conventional medical treatments. His work enhanced cultural competence among healthcare providers, provided better healthcare access for the Indigenous community, and provided a model program for integrating traditional and modern healthcare practices.

As demonstrated by the example of a global company trying to grow in East Asia, cultural booking may be essential in the business sector. Sarah, a cultural broker with expertise in East Asian markets and cultures, was brought on board to guide the expansion process. She conducted cultural competence training for the company's executives and was crucial in negotiating business agreements that respected local customs and business practices. Her insights into the cultural nuances of business communication and her ability to navigate complex negotiations were instrumental in the company's successful expansion, fostering beneficial partnerships and avoiding costly missteps.

The final case study highlights the power of cultural brokerage in community development projects. A neighborhood with a diverse population, including refugees and migrants, faced challenges in community integration and access to services. Ahmed, a respected figure in the community with a background in social work, acted as a cultural broker to facilitate dialogue and collaboration between community members and local government. He organized multicultural festivals, community forums, and language exchange programs, creating spaces for shared experiences and mutual learning. Ahmed's efforts led to establishing community-led initiatives that addressed local needs, from youth mentorship programs to multicultural community centers, strengthening the neighborhood's social fabric.

These case studies underscore the multifaceted role of cultural brokers in creating positive change. Whether in education, healthcare, business, or community development, cultural brokers leverage their skills and characteristics to foster environments where diverse perspectives are valued and harnessed for mutual benefit. Their work goes beyond mere translation or mediation; it involves deep empathy, cultural competence, and navigating complex social dynamics. By highlighting successful examples of cultural brokerage, these case studies offer valuable lessons on understanding, respect, and collaboration in overcoming cultural barriers and building more robust, inclusive communities.

CHAPTER 4

DR. OSCAR HARRIS'S STUDY: A PHENOMENOLOGICAL PERSPECTIVE ON EPSTEIN'S FRAMEWORK

Epstein's framework of parental involvement provides a comprehensive model for understanding and enhancing the collaboration between schools, families, and communities to support children's learning and development. Developed by Dr. Joyce Epstein and her colleagues at Johns Hopkins University, the framework identifies six types of parental involvement that can contribute to positive educational outcomes. This model serves as a blueprint for educators, policymakers, and families, emphasizing the multifaceted role of parental engagement in the educational process.

The first type, **parenting,** involves helping families establish home environments that support children as students. Schools can offer parenting workshops or information on child development and learning strategies, fostering an atmosphere conducive to education beyond the school premises.

The **second type of communication** focuses on developing effective channels for school-to-home and home-to-school communication. This includes ensuring that families are informed about school policies, programs, and their children's progress in a timely and accessible manner. It underscores the importance of two-way communication, where parents' questions and concerns are welcomed and addressed.

The third type, **volunteering,** encourages parents and family members to support the school through their participation and assistance. This can range from volunteering in the classroom to participating in school governance. The aim is to enhance the educational experience by leveraging the community's skills and expertise.

Learning at home, the fourth type, emphasizes the importance of families in children's learning by providing information and ideas to families about how to help with homework and other curriculum-related activities. This framework seeks to extend learning opportunities beyond the school and engage families in the educational process.

The fifth type, **decision-making,** includes families in school decisions and the development of parent leaders and representatives. This type encourages schools to involve parents in advisory roles, committees, and policy-making processes, recognizing the valuable insights and perspectives they bring.

Finally, **collaborating with the community** identifies ways schools can coordinate resources and services from the community for families, students, and the school, and vice versa. This type encourages partnerships with local businesses, organizations, and public services to enrich the learning environment and provide additional student support.

Epstein's framework highlights the dynamic and reciprocal relationship between schools and families, advocating for a partnership that recognizes the integral role of parental involvement in student success. It presents a holistic approach to engagement that goes beyond academic support to include health, welfare, and community involvement. By utilizing this approach, educational institutions may establish more effective, encouraging, and inclusive learning environments that meet the varied needs of both students and their families. This model facilitates academic achievement and nurtures well-rounded individuals who are connected to and supported by their communities.

Oscar Harris's study

Dr. Oscar Harris's study delves into the practical application of Epstein's framework for parental involvement, mainly focusing on its implementation within middle schools serving English Language Learner (ELL) populations in the Pacific Northwest. The research aims to uncover the lived experiences of ELL teachers and language specialists as they navigate the challenges and opportunities of engaging parents in their children's education. Harris's work is pivotal in understanding how Epstein's theoretical model translates into real-world practices, especially in the context of cultural and linguistic diversity.

Through a phenomenological approach, Harris explores the nuanced ways educators facilitate parental involvement across Epstein's six types, shedding light on the most effective strategies and the barriers that impede progress. The study is grounded in the belief that parental engagement is a critical factor in student academic success, yet recognizes that ELL families may face unique challenges in becoming involved due to language barriers, cultural differences, and other factors.

In-depth interviews with educators are vital to Harris's research methodology since they enable them to share their observations, opinions, and experiences. This qualitative approach provides a rich, detailed understanding of the complexities of implementing Epstein's framework in a diverse educational landscape. It highlights the innovative practices teachers and language specialists employ to bridge communication gaps, foster cultural understanding and actively involve ELL parents in the school community.

A significant study finding is the crucial role of cultural competence and sensitivity in engaging ELL families. Educators must navigate language barriers and respect and incorporate diverse cultural backgrounds into their engagement strategies. Harris points to the need for schools to act as cultural brokers, facilitating a two-way understanding and appreciation between diverse family backgrounds and the school's educational culture.

Dr. Oscar Harris's study contributes valuable insights to educational research, particularly in highlighting the adaptability of Epstein's framework in diverse settings. It underscores the importance of personalized, culturally aware approaches to parental involvement. It calls for further research and training to equip educators with the skills necessary to engage effectively with ELL families. Harris's work emphasizes that successful parental involvement is not a one-size-fits-all endeavor. Still, it requires a deep understanding of and respect for each family's unique challenges and strengths.

Key findings and implications for school-community partnerships

Dr. Oscar Harris's study on the application of Epstein's parental involvement framework within schools serving English Language Learner (ELL) populations yields key findings that have significant implications for the development and strengthening of school-community partnerships. These insights highlight the nuances of engaging diverse communities and underscore the need for inclusive and adaptive approaches.

Key Findings

1. Cultural Competence is Crucial: One central finding is the importance of cultural competence among educators. The study reveals that successful engagement with ELL families requires an understanding and appreciating their diverse cultural backgrounds. Teachers and language specialists who demonstrate cultural sensitivity are more effective in building trust and fostering meaningful communication with parents.

2. Barriers to Engagement: Harris identifies several barriers to parental involvement, including language differences, unfamiliarity with the educational system, and varying cultural expectations about parental roles in education. These barriers necessitate targeted strategies to facilitate engagement and ensure all families can contribute to their children's education.

3. The Role of Cultural Brokers: The study highlights the effectiveness of employing cultural brokers, individuals who facilitate communication and understanding between the school and ELL families. Cultural brokers can help overcome barriers to engagement by providing translation services, explaining educational practices, and mediating cultural misunderstandings.

4. Communication Strategies: Effective communication strategies are critical for engaging ELL families. This includes providing information in multiple languages, using various communication channels, and ensuring two-way communication, allowing parents to share their insights and concerns.

5. Tailored Engagement Approaches: No one-size-fits-all approach to engaging ELL families exists. The study emphasizes the need for personalized engagement strategies that consider different families' specific needs, preferences, and challenges. This may involve home visits, community meetings, or the creation of parent advisory groups.

Implications for School-Community Partnerships

1. Training in Cultural Competence: Schools should prioritize professional development opportunities for educators focusing on building cultural competence. This training can equip teachers with the skills necessary to engage effectively with diverse communities and foster inclusive educational environments.

2. Investing in Cultural Brokers: School-community partnerships should consider investing in cultural brokers to enhance engagement with ELL families. Cultural mediators can strengthen the bond between schools and communities by overcoming linguistic and cultural divides.

3. Adaptive Communication Methods: Partnerships should adopt flexible and adaptive communication methods that cater to the community's linguistic and cultural diversity. This might include translating materials into multiple languages, using visual aids, and employing technology to facilitate communication.

4. Community Engagement Initiatives: Schools should collaborate with community organizations that are experts in working with diverse populations. These collaborations can offer helpful tools and assistance for interacting with ELL families and enhancing the educational process for every student.

5. Evaluation and Feedback: Ongoing evaluation of parental involvement strategies and feedback from ELL families are essential for continuous improvement. Schools should establish mechanisms for regularly assessing the effectiveness of their engagement efforts and making necessary adjustments.

Dr. Oscar Harris's study illuminates the complex dynamics of engaging ELL families within school-community partnerships. The research's main conclusions and recommendations highlight the need for a sophisticated, culturally sensitive approach to parental participation. By embracing these strategies, schools can foster stronger partnerships with all segments of their communities, enhancing educational outcomes and promoting a more inclusive society.

Application of findings in real-world contexts

Applying the findings from research on effective engagement with English Language Learner (ELL) families and cultural brokerage in real-world educational contexts requires a multifaceted approach that considers the nuances of cultural, linguistic, and educational dynamics. The insights from such studies, including those by Dr. Oscar Harris on Epstein's parental involvement framework, offer valuable strategies for educators, administrators, and policymakers to foster more inclusive, effective school-community partnerships. Here's how these findings can be translated into practice:

Developing Cultural Competency Training Programs

Schools should implement comprehensive cultural competency training for all staff members, including teachers, administrators, and support staff. This training would cover understanding diverse cultural backgrounds, effective communication strategies, and culturally responsive teaching practices. Schools may provide a welcoming, respectful, and valued environment for all families by raising staff understanding and sensitivity.

Establishing Roles for Cultural Brokers

Recognizing the importance of cultural brokers, schools should establish formal roles for individuals—whether staff members, community volunteers, or hired professionals—who can navigate cultural and linguistic divides. These cultural brokers would work directly with ELL families, providing translation services, facilitating communication with educators, and helping to navigate the educational system. Their role would also include educating school staff on the unique needs and strengths of the ELL community.

Enhancing Communication Strategies

To address the communication barriers identified in the research, schools need to adopt more versatile and accessible communication methods. This could include providing school materials in multiple languages, using visual aids and simple language to ensure comprehension, and leveraging technology—such as mobile apps and social media—to reach families where they are. Schools could also establish regular, informal events, like coffee mornings or cultural celebration days, to foster direct, face-to-face communication in a relaxed setting.

Personalizing Family Engagement Efforts

Given the diversity within ELL populations, personalized approaches to family engagement are critical. Schools could conduct surveys or interviews to understand different families' specific preferences, needs, and challenges. Based on this information, tailored programs or initiatives could be developed, ranging from home visits for families unable to attend school meetings to setting up parent-led groups that reflect the community's diverse interests and languages.

Leveraging Community Partnerships

Partnerships with community organizations with experience and expertise in working with diverse populations can significantly enhance a school's engagement efforts. These organizations can offer ELL families resources, knowledge, and direct support. Collaborations might include:

- Community-based educational programs.

- Language learning resources.
- Cultural events that celebrate and integrate the student body's diverse backgrounds.

Incorporating Technology Thoughtfully

While technology can bridge many gaps in communication and learning, its implementation must be thoughtful and inclusive. Schools should ensure that digital tools and resources are accessible to all families, including those with limited internet access or digital literacy. This might involve training parents on digital platforms, lending devices to needy families, and creating offline alternatives to ensure no one is left behind.

Creating Feedback Loops

To continually improve engagement strategies, schools should establish mechanisms for gathering feedback from ELL families and cultural brokers. This could involve regular surveys, suggestion boxes, and feedback sessions. Schools must be prepared to act on this feedback, demonstrating to families that their voices are heard and valued.

Advocating for Policy Support

Finally, applying these findings in real-world contexts requires supportive policies at the district, state, and national levels. Advocacy efforts could focus on securing funding for cultural competency training, technology access for ELL families, and establishing cultural broker roles within schools. Policymakers should be informed of the research findings and the positive impact of these strategies on student outcomes.

By applying these research findings in real-world educational contexts, schools can significantly improve their engagement with ELL families. This leads to better student academic outcomes and more robust, cohesive school communities. These strategies represent a commitment to inclusivity, respect, and partnership, laying the groundwork for an educational environment where every student and family can thrive.

CHAPTER 5

Establishing effective communication channels between schools and their communities is a cornerstone for nurturing fruitful partnerships that significantly enhance educational experiences and outcomes. In today's diverse and fast-paced world, crafting these channels requires more than just sending out a monthly newsletter or holding annual parent-teacher meetings. It demands a strategic, inclusive, multifaceted approach to ensure every community member feels informed, involved, and heard.

The first step in this process is recognizing the diversity within the school community. Schools are microcosms of society, encompassing families from varied cultural, linguistic, and socio-economic backgrounds. Acknowledging this diversity means adopting communication strategies that are accessible to all. This could involve providing translation services for non-English speaking families, using simple language free of educational jargon, and utilizing various communication mediums to reach different audiences. From traditional letters home to digital platforms such as school websites, social media, and SMS alerts, the goal is to meet community members where they are.

Moreover, effective communication is not just about disseminating information but also about fostering a two-way dialogue. Creating avenues for feedback, questions, and discussions encourages active participation from families and community members. This could be facilitated through regular community forums, suggestion boxes, online surveys, or interactive social media posts. Schools that listen to their communities and adapt based on their feedback are more likely to build trust and engagement, leading to stronger partnerships.

Another crucial aspect is ensuring regularity and consistency in communication. Whether it's weekly updates from the principal, monthly newsletters from teachers, or daily posts on the school's social media channels, establishing a predictable rhythm helps set expectations and builds a habit of engagement. Consistency also applies to the tone and quality of the communication, which should always be respectful, professional, and reflective of the school's values.

Effective communication channels can provide regular updates on school events, achievements, and initiatives, share educational resources, highlight community services, and provide learning support tips for families. By extending the scope of communication beyond administrative news to include valuable content for student learning and well-being, schools can further cement their role as critical educational resources within the community.

Engaging community leaders and organizations in the communication process can amplify the school's message and reach wider audiences. Partnerships with local businesses, cultural institutions, and service organizations can lead to collaborative projects and mutually beneficial events. By sharing these stories through the school's communication channels, schools showcase the strength of their community ties and open up new avenues for involvement and support.

Schools need to utilize data and technology effectively when implementing these strategies. Analytics from digital communication platforms can provide insights into which types of content engage families the most, the best times to post updates, and how different community segments prefer to receive information. This data-driven approach allows schools to tailor their communication strategies for maximum impact.

Equally important is training for school staff on effective communication practices. Educators, administrators, and support staff are critical in building relationships with families and community members. Professional development opportunities focusing on cultural competency, communication skills, and community engagement can empower staff to contribute positively to the school's communication efforts.

Establishing effective communication channels is a dynamic and ongoing process that requires thoughtfulness, creativity, and commitment. Schools can build robust communication systems that support strong, vibrant school-community partnerships by embracing diversity, fostering two-way dialogue, maintaining regularity and consistency, sharing valuable content, leveraging community partnerships, utilizing data and technology, and investing in staff training.

The collaborations above foster an atmosphere conducive to students' intellectual, social, and emotional well-being, highlighting the significant influence of communication on education.

Facilitating collaboration and engagement

Facilitating collaboration and engagement within school-community partnerships is akin to nurturing a garden. It's about planting seeds of cooperation, watering them with consistent communication, and providing enough sunlight through shared goals and visions to see them grow into fruitful outcomes. This process, essential for enriching educational experiences, requires a hands-on, thoughtful approach to bringing together diverse members of the school and the broader community in meaningful ways.

The bedrock of facilitating effective collaboration is the establishment of a common purpose. Schools and community members must identify shared goals that resonate with everyone involved. Whether enhancing student literacy, supporting STEM education, or promoting physical well-being, having a clear, mutual objective sets the direction for collaborative efforts. This common purpose is a rallying point, encouraging various stakeholders to contribute their unique strengths and resources towards achieving shared outcomes.

Another critical element is creating inclusive spaces for engagement. Schools must ensure that all voices are heard and valued, especially those from underrepresented or marginalized groups. This might involve hosting meetings at times that are convenient for working parents, providing childcare during events, or using technology to affect those who cannot be physically present. The goal is to reduce obstacles to involvement so that everyone can participate more easily.

Moreover, recognizing and celebrating the diversity within the community can enrich collaboration efforts. Schools can host cultural fairs, art exhibitions, and storytelling nights that showcase different community members' traditions, languages, and experiences. These events foster a sense of belonging and appreciation among students and families and provide rich, real-world learning opportunities that complement the academic curriculum.

Building trust is another cornerstone of facilitating engagement. Trust is cultivated over time through consistent, open communication, transparency in decision-making, and a demonstrated commitment to acting on community feedback. Schools can foster trust by regularly updating the community on partnership activities, celebrating successes, and openly discussing challenges and lessons learned. When trust is established, collaboration becomes more fluid, and community members are more likely to invest their time, energy, and resources.

Collaboration is further improved when community members assume leadership positions within partnership projects. Schools can develop a cadre of community leaders who can spearhead projects, mobilize resources, and advocate for the partnership's goals by providing training and support. Empowered individuals bring new energy and perspectives, driving innovation and ensuring that initiatives remain responsive to the community's needs.

The use of technology also plays a pivotal role in facilitating collaboration and engagement. Digital platforms can be a hub for sharing information, coordinating activities, and celebrating achievements. They provide a forum for continuous discussion where suggestions can be shared, and criticism can be effectively obtained. Additionally, social media can reach broader audiences, highlight partnership successes, and attract new participants and resources.

To sustain engagement over the long term, it's essential to evaluate the impact of collaboration efforts regularly. This involves collecting data on how partnership initiatives affect student learning, community well-being, and other vital outcomes. Sharing these results with the community demonstrates the value of their contributions and informs future planning and decision-making. Regular evaluation also provides an opportunity to adjust strategies as needed, ensuring the partnership remains dynamic and responsive to changing needs.

Finally, celebrating successes, no matter how small, is crucial for maintaining momentum and enthusiasm. Recognizing the contributions of all participants, from students and teachers to families and community partners, reinforces the importance of everyone's involvement. Celebrations can be simple acknowledgments in school newsletters, awards ceremonies, or public thank-you at community events. These gestures of appreciation build a positive culture around the partnership, encouraging ongoing commitment and support.

Facilitating collaboration and engagement in school-community partnerships is a multifaceted process that requires deliberate planning, inclusive practices, and a commitment to building trust and mutual respect. Schools can cultivate vibrant partnerships that enhance educational outcomes and strengthen community ties by uniting around a common purpose, creating inclusive spaces for participation, celebrating diversity, empowering community leaders, leveraging technology, evaluating impact, and celebrating successes. This collaborative spirit, nurtured carefully over time, can transform educational experiences, making them more prosperous, more meaningful, and reflective of the diverse communities they serve.

Building trust and mutual understanding

Building trust and mutual understanding is akin to laying the foundation for a house that everyone in the community helps to make—a home where every brick represents a shared experience, every window offers a glimpse into diverse perspectives, and every door opens to collaboration and respect. This foundational work is crucial in creating an environment where school-community partnerships can flourish, leading to enriched educational experiences and more robust, cohesive communities.

The foundation of any successful collaboration is trust. It's built over time through consistent, honest interactions and by demonstrating reliability and integrity. In school-community partnerships, building trust starts with open and transparent communication. Schools must share their successes, challenges, and failures with the community. This openness shows a willingness to be vulnerable, a critical step in fostering trust. When community members see that schools are honest about their limitations and are actively seeking solutions, they are more likely to offer their support and understanding.

Mutual understanding is equally important. It requires truly listening to and comprehending all stakeholders' perspectives, values, and needs. For schools, this means learning about the community's cultural backgrounds, economic conditions, and social dynamics. Engaging in active listening—where the goal is to understand rather than respond—can reveal insights about making educational experiences more relevant and meaningful for students and their families. Similarly, community members are encouraged to understand schools' challenges and constraints, creating a more empathetic and supportive environment.

Schools can organize events and activities that unite different community members in informal settings to foster mutual understanding. Workshops, cultural exchange events, and community service projects are excellent opportunities for people to interact, share stories, and learn from one another. These interactions help to break down stereotypes and build personal connections, making it easier to work together towards common goals.

Consistency is another essential component in developing trust. Schools and community leaders must continue their commitments and maintain their efforts over time. Whether regularly updating the community on the progress of joint projects, consistently seeking feedback on school policies, or reliably offering support services to families, consistent actions demonstrate commitment and reliability, further strengthening trust.

Acknowledging and gratitude significantly aid mutual understanding and trust. It shows that community members' contributions, whether they are volunteers, parents, or local business owners, are valued.

Simple acts of recognition, like thank-you notes, public acknowledgments, or awards, can make people feel appreciated and more deeply connected to the partnership.

Resolving conflicts respectfully and constructively is also crucial. Disagreements are inevitable in any partnership, but handling them can strengthen or weaken trust. Schools and community members must approach conflicts with an open mind, be willing to find common ground and be committed to achieving a resolution respecting everyone's interests. This approach resolves the immediate issue and builds resilience and trust in the partnership's ability to overcome challenges.

Flexibility and adaptability are essential in maintaining trust and mutual understanding. As communities evolve and new challenges arise, school-community partnerships must be willing to adjust their strategies and approaches. Responding to changing needs and being open to innovation demonstrates a commitment to collaboration and to continuously improving educational experiences.

Building trust and mutual understanding is a dynamic and ongoing process at the heart of successful school-community partnerships. It calls for polite dispute settlement, constant behavior, attentive listening, open and honest communication, and the adaptability to take on new tasks. By prioritizing these principles, schools and communities can lay a strong foundation for collaboration, leading to inclusive, supportive educational environments that reflect all stakeholders' diverse needs and strengths. This foundational trust and understanding enhance students' academic experiences and contribute to building more robust, more connected communities.

Leveraging resources and community assets

Leveraging resources and community assets is a strategic approach that can significantly enhance students' educational experiences while strengthening the community's fabric. It's about recognizing and utilizing the resources, skills, knowledge, and strengths available within a community to support and enrich the school's educational programs. This collaborative strategy maximizes the impact of available resources and fosters a sense of shared responsibility and investment in students' success.

The first step in leveraging these assets is to conduct a thorough asset mapping of the community. This involves identifying the various resources available within the community, such as local businesses, cultural institutions, public libraries, parks and recreation centers, universities, and non-profit organizations. Understanding what each entity can offer, from expertise and physical spaces to volunteers and financial support, provides a clear picture of the potential partnerships that can be developed to support educational goals.

Once the assets have been identified, the next step is to build and strengthen relationships with these community stakeholders. This involves reaching out to potential partners, sharing the school's vision and goals, and discussing how collaboration can be mutually beneficial. It's essential to approach these relationships with reciprocity, recognizing that partnerships should provide value to all parties involved. Whether it's a local business providing internships for students, a museum offering educational programs, or a university sharing research facilities, each partnership should be designed to meet the needs of the students while also benefiting the community partner.

Effective collaboration also requires coordination and communication to ensure that resources and assets are utilized efficiently and effectively. This might involve creating a coordinating body or committee that includes representatives from the school and various community partners. This committee can oversee the implementation of partnership activities, monitor progress, and adjust plans to ensure that resources are used most effectively.

An example of leveraging community assets effectively is the partnership between schools and local libraries. Libraries can offer students many resources, including books, technology, and learning programs. By collaborating with libraries, schools can extend learning opportunities beyond the classroom, offering students access to summer reading programs, homework help sessions, and STEM workshops. This partnership enriches the student's learning experience and increases their engagement with the library, reinforcing its role as a valuable community resource.

Another example is collaboration with local businesses and industries. Through these collaborations, students can take advantage of real-world learning experiences, including internships, job shadowing, and mentoring programs. These experiences help students better understand the range of professional options available and helpful information and abilities they can use immediately in the workplace. For businesses, these partnerships help shape future employees who are better prepared and more aligned with the skills and competencies needed in the industry.

Acknowledging and using families' and parents' abilities and skills while utilizing community resources is crucial. Parents can offer a range of skills, from professional expertise to cultural knowledge, that can enrich the educational experience. Schools can engage parents by inviting them to share their skills and knowledge through guest lectures, career days, or cultural celebrations. This enhances the curriculum and strengthens the school's and families' connection, building a more supportive and engaged community.

To maximize the impact of these partnerships, it's crucial to evaluate their effectiveness regularly. This involves collecting feedback from students, teachers, parents, and community partners to assess the collaboration's benefits and identify areas for improvement. Frequent assessment guarantees that the collaborations stay pertinent and satisfy the changing requirements of the community and students.

Leveraging resources and community assets is a powerful strategy for enhancing students' educational experiences while fostering a strong and supportive community. By conducting asset mapping, building reciprocal relationships, coordinating efforts, and regularly evaluating impact, schools can create dynamic partnerships that bring students a wealth of resources, expertise, and opportunities. These collaborations support students' academic and personal development and strengthen the community, creating a vibrant ecosystem where education is a shared responsibility. Every member plays a role in supporting the next generation's success.

CHAPTER 6

Developing partnerships between schools and communities can sometimes feel like navigating a maze with no apparent exit. While the goal of enhancing student learning and community engagement is well-defined, the path to get there is often littered with obstacles. Acknowledging these obstacles is the initial phase in formulating efficacious tactics to surmount them and facilitate triumphant cooperation.

One common obstacle is a need for clear communication. Just as in any relationship, communication is critical to understanding and cooperation. Misunderstandings can arise without clear channels and consistent messages, leading to frustration and distrust. Working with various populations might worsen this problem since language limitations can make communication more difficult. Ensuring all parties have access to information and understand each other's expectations is crucial for developing strong partnerships.

Another significant challenge is differing expectations and goals. Schools and community organizations often partner with their own sets of objectives. While schools may focus on academic achievement and student well-being, community partners might prioritize exposure to real-world experiences or promoting specific skills. Aligning these different expectations requires open dialogue and flexibility from all parties involved.

Resource constraints also pose a considerable challenge. Schools and community organizations operate with limited budgets, staff, and time, making initiating and sustaining partnership activities difficult. While the enthusiasm for collaboration is often there, the practical means to implement plans still need to be improved. Finding creative solutions and leveraging existing resources can help mitigate these constraints, but they remain a significant hurdle for many partnerships.

Trust and mutual respect can be another obstacle in developing effective partnerships. Building trust takes time and is founded on consistent, positive interactions. However, past experiences of failed collaborations or unmet expectations can lead to skepticism and reluctance to engage in new partnerships. Overcoming this barrier requires patience, transparency, and a demonstrated commitment to the partnership's success.

Cultural differences and lack of cultural competence can also hinder the development of school-community partnerships. Schools serve increasingly diverse student populations, making it essential for schools and community partners to understand and appreciate different cultures deeply. Without this understanding, there's a risk of cultural insensitivity or misinterpretation of intentions, which can alienate community members and impede the partnership's development.

Engaging all stakeholders is another common challenge. While some community members may be highly active and engaged, others may be difficult to reach or reluctant to participate. This can lead to an imbalance in involvement and representation, which might skew the partnership's focus and outcomes. Ensuring that all voices are heard and valued is essential for the partnership's inclusivity and effectiveness.

Lastly, implementing partnership projects might be slowed down or prevented by overcoming regulatory restrictions and bureaucratic roadblocks. Schools and community organizations often operate under different sets of rules and regulations, which can limit what can be done within the framework of a partnership. Finding common ground that complies with all regulatory requirements while achieving the partnership's goals can be complex and time-consuming.

All parties participating in the collaboration must work together to overcome these challenges. It necessitates imagination, adaptability, and a readiness to face and overcome obstacles together. By acknowledging and actively addressing these common obstacles, schools and community organizations can build stronger, more effective partnerships that benefit students and the wider community. The journey might be fraught with challenges, but the rewards—a more engaged, educated, and cohesive community—are well worth the effort.

Addressing cultural, linguistic, and systemic barriers

Addressing the trio of cultural, linguistic, and systemic barriers in the context of school-community partnerships is akin to navigating a complex labyrinth. These barriers can significantly hinder the development and success of such collaborations. Still, they can be overcome with thoughtful strategies and persistent efforts, paving the way for more inclusive and effective partnerships.

Cultural barriers often emerge from a need for more understanding and appreciation of the diverse backgrounds and traditions that students and their families bring to the educational environment. Schools are vibrant tapestries woven from myriad cultural threads, and recognizing this diversity is the first step toward addressing cultural barriers. Including cultural competency training for educators and staff, ensuring that the curriculum represents the diversity of the student body, and planning multicultural events that encourage community members to engage and learn about one another's cultures are some strategies used to address this. By cultivating an atmosphere of tolerance and understanding for cultural variety, schools may strengthen and expand the reach of their communities.

Linguistic barriers present another significant challenge, particularly in schools serving families for whom English is not the first language. These barriers can prevent effective communication between the school and home, hindering parent engagement and students' academic progress. To address this, schools can offer translation and interpretation services for critical communications, parent-teacher meetings, and school events. Additionally, embracing bilingual education and support programs can not only aid in overcoming linguistic barriers but also enrich the learning environment for all students by fostering multilingual skills and cultural awareness.

Systemic barriers are the most daunting, rooted in policies, practices, and societal structures that inadvertently disadvantage certain groups. These barriers can manifest in various forms, from unequal access to educational resources to biases in disciplinary practices. Tackling systemic barriers requires a multifaceted approach, beginning with a thorough assessment to identify inequities within the school system. To identify patterns of imbalance, data on discipline, resource distribution by demographic groupings, and student achievement must be gathered and evaluated. Based on these findings, schools can develop targeted strategies to address identified issues, such as reallocating resources to underserved areas, implementing restorative justice practices to replace exclusionary discipline, and adopting policies that ensure equitable treatment for all students.

Engaging the broader community is crucial in addressing cultural, linguistic, and systemic barriers. Community organizations, local businesses, and cultural institutions can offer invaluable resources, expertise, and support. Partnerships with these entities can provide students with additional learning opportunities, mentorship programs, and access to services that may not be available within the school. Moreover, involving community members in decision-making ensures that diverse perspectives are considered when developing and implementing school policies and programs.

Innovation and flexibility are crucial to overcoming these barriers. Schools must be willing to explore new approaches and adapt existing practices better to meet the needs of their diverse student populations. This might involve leveraging technology to enhance communication and learning opportunities, rethinking scheduling and staffing to provide more personalized support to students, or adopting more culturally responsive teaching methods.

Continuous evaluation and reflection are essential to successfully addressing cultural, linguistic, and systemic barriers. Schools should establish mechanisms for regular monitoring of their efforts to ensure they are making progress toward greater inclusivity and equity. Comments from kids, families, and community partners can point out areas that still need work and offer insightful information about these initiatives' benefits.

Addressing cultural, linguistic, and systemic barriers in school-community partnerships is an ongoing challenge that requires commitment, creativity, and collaboration. By recognizing and valuing the diversity within their communities, schools can develop strategies that overcome these barriers and enhance the educational experience for all students. This work is not easy, and progress may be slow, but the benefits of creating a more inclusive, equitable, and supportive educational environment are immeasurable. Through concerted effort and dedication, schools can transform these challenges into opportunities for growth, learning, and stronger community connections.

Strategies for navigating power dynamics and conflicts

Navigating power dynamics and conflicts within school-community partnerships requires a blend of tact, understanding, and strategic planning. These dynamics often reflect broader societal inequalities and can lead to tension and misunderstandings. However, with suitable approaches, creating a more balanced and harmonious environment conducive to effective collaboration is possible.

Firstly, recognizing and acknowledging the existence of power imbalances is crucial. Various factors, including economic status, race, education, and language proficiency, can influence power dynamics. Schools need to be proactive in identifying these imbalances and addressing them head-on. This might involve creating spaces where all voices, especially those of marginalized or less powerful community members, are heard and valued. Listening sessions, focus groups, and anonymous feedback mechanisms can ensure everyone has a say in the partnership's direction.

Building mutual respect and trust is another essential strategy. This goes beyond mere acknowledgment of power disparities to actively working to build relationships based on mutual respect. Schools and community leaders can foster this environment by consistently demonstrating reliability, openness, and a genuine commitment to the partnership's goals. Celebrating small wins together, recognizing contributions, and sharing credit can also strengthen trust and respect among all stakeholders.

Resolving disputes and power dynamics requires effective communication. Clear, transparent, and inclusive communication can help prevent misunderstandings that may lead to conflicts. Schools should clearly communicate their intentions, plans, and actions and provide regular updates on the partnership's progress. Using a range of communication channels also guarantees that information is available to all people, regardless of their preferred method of communication.

Conflict resolution mechanisms are vital for managing disputes that arise. Despite best efforts, conflicts are inevitable in any partnership. Establishing clear, fair, and transparent procedures for resolving disputes can help manage these situations effectively. Mediation by a neutral third party, regular conflict resolution training for staff and community leaders, and clear conflict resolution guidelines can provide a framework for constructively resolving conflicts.

Empowering all partners by distributing leadership and decision-making roles can also help balance power dynamics. This means involving community members in planning, decision-making, and evaluation processes. By sharing leadership, schools can demonstrate their commitment to genuinely collaborative partnerships where all stakeholders have a stake in the partnership's success.

Another critical strategy is providing education and training on power dynamics, cultural competence, and conflict resolution. Workshops, seminars, and ongoing professional development opportunities can equip teachers, staff, community leaders, and members with the skills and knowledge to navigate complex power dynamics and resolve conflicts effectively. This education can also help participants recognize their biases and assumptions, which is crucial for building more equitable and inclusive partnerships.

Celebrating diversity and fostering an inclusive environment is essential for mitigating power imbalances. Acknowledging and appreciating the distinct contributions of many languages, cultures, and viewpoints may improve collaboration and aid in dismantling power structures. Cultural events, multicultural education programs, and inclusive decision-making processes can highlight the value of diversity within the school and community.

Finally, continuous reflection and adaptation are necessary for effectively navigating power dynamics and conflicts. Schools and community partners should regularly reflect on their practices, seeking feedback from all stakeholders and being willing to make changes based on what they learn. This reflective practice can help partnerships evolve and adapt to new challenges, ensuring they remain responsive to the needs of all involved.

Navigating power dynamics and conflicts in school-community partnerships requires a multifaceted approach prioritizing equity, respect, and collaboration. By acknowledging power imbalances, building trust, communicating effectively, establishing conflict resolution mechanisms, distributing leadership, providing education and training, celebrating diversity, and continuously reflecting and adapting, schools and communities can work together more harmoniously. These strategies help manage power dynamics and conflicts and strengthen the partnership, benefiting students and the wider community.

Case studies highlighting successful resolution of challenges

Exploring case studies highlighting the successful resolution of challenges in school-community partnerships offers invaluable lessons and inspiration for those navigating similar paths. These real-world examples demonstrate how creativity, collaboration, and commitment can turn potential roadblocks into stepping stones toward more robust, more effective partnerships.

Case Study 1: Bridging Language Barriers

A primary school in a diverse urban district faced significant challenges engaging non-English-speaking families. Having realized family engagement is essential to a student's development, the school implemented a multilingual communication plan. They employed bilingual staff members, developed a multilingual website, and provided interpreters for school events and meetings. Furthermore, the school launched a series of cultural exchange nights where families shared their traditions and languages with the school community. This approach improved communication with non-English-speaking families and enriched the school's cultural awareness, leading to a more inclusive environment.

Case Study 2: Overcoming Resource Limitations

A rural school needed more access to STEM (Science, Technology, Engineering, and Mathematics) resources, hindering its ability to provide a comprehensive STEM curriculum. The school partnered with a local university and several tech companies to address this. The university provided access to labs and guest lecturers, while the tech companies donated equipment and facilitated workshops for students. This collaborative effort enhanced the school's STEM offerings and exposed students to real-world applications of their studies and potential career paths in the tech industry.

Case Study 3: Resolving Conflicts through Mediation

When a new sports program led to conflicts between the school and a segment of the community who felt the program was diverting funds from academic pursuits, the school sought to address the issue through a structured mediation process. They organized a series of community forums facilitated by a professional mediator where all parties could voice their concerns and suggestions. Through these discussions, it became clear that the community's primary concern was maintaining a balanced focus on academics. In response, the school proposed a plan to bolster academic programs through partnerships with local businesses and universities while continuing the sports program. The issue was resolved, and a more involved and encouraging community resulted from this well-received compromise.

Case Study 4: Addressing Cultural Misunderstandings

In a school with a growing number of immigrant students, cultural misunderstandings between teachers and students' families were leading to decreased family engagement. The school responded by implementing a series of cultural competency workshops for teachers and staff, focusing on the cultures represented in the student body. The school invited families to share their artistic practices and perspectives through classroom presentations and school-wide cultural festivals. These initiatives fostered a deeper understanding and respect for diverse cultures within the school community, improving relationships and increasing family engagement.

Case Study 5: Leveraging Community Assets for Extracurricular Programs

Facing budget cuts that threatened the continuation of its arts and music programs, a school identified local artists and musicians willing to volunteer their time to teach classes and lead extracurricular activities. The school also partnered with a community center to host performances and art exhibits. This approach saved the arts and music programs and strengthened ties with the local arts community, providing students with enriching experiences and mentorship opportunities. These case studies illustrate that challenges in school-community partnerships are inevitable but possible. Schools and communities can find innovative solutions that benefit students and strengthen partnerships through open communication, creative problem-solving, and a commitment to collaboration. These examples testify to the power of collective effort and its positive impact on the educational landscape.

CHAPTER 7

CULTIVATING SUSTAINABLE PARTNERSHIPS

reating a culture of partnership within schools and communities is akin to cultivating a garden where every plant and flower thrives, contributing to a vibrant and healthy ecosystem. This culture doesn't sprout overnight; it grows from the seeds of mutual respect, shared goals, and continuous nurturing. When schools and communities come together in true partnership, they create an environment where students flourish academically, socially, and emotionally.

The foundation of this culture is built on mutual respect and understanding. Recognizing each stakeholder's inherent value and contributions, from parents and teachers to local businesses and community organizations, sets the stage for meaningful collaboration. Schools must take the initiative to reach out, listen actively, and engage with the community in a way that acknowledges its diversity and potential.

Establishing shared goals is crucial. When schools and communities align their objectives, focusing on the holistic development of students and the community's well-being, they set a common direction for their efforts. These goals range from improving literacy rates and providing extracurricular opportunities to addressing local social issues and enhancing community spaces. Shared goals serve as a rallying point, uniting schools and communities to pursue positive outcomes.

Communication is the lifeline of a thriving partnership culture. Transparent, open, consistent communication channels ensure everyone is informed, involved, and invested. Schools can use various tools and platforms to reach a wider audience, from traditional newsletters and community meetings to social media and mobile apps. Establishing forums for discussion where community members may express their thoughts, worries, and goals is equally vital. All parties involved benefit from this two-way communication by feeling a sense of ownership and belonging.

Another critical element is empowering individuals to participate actively in the partnership process. This involves providing parents, students, and community members opportunities to lead initiatives, participate in decision-making, and contribute their skills and knowledge. When people feel empowered, they are more engaged and motivated to contribute to the partnership's success. Schools can facilitate this by offering leadership training, recognizing and celebrating contributions, and creating flexible roles accommodating diverse talents and schedules.

Building trust takes time and consistency. Trust grows from seeing words turned into actions, commitments fulfilled, and positive impacts on students and the community. Schools and community partners must demonstrate reliability, follow through on promises, and show genuine concern for each other's well-being. Trust is the glue that holds the partnership together, enabling stakeholders to navigate challenges and conflicts with confidence in each other's support.

Adapting to change and being open to innovation is essential in maintaining a vibrant partnership culture. As communities evolve and new challenges arise, schools and community partners must be willing to reassess their approaches, experiment with new ideas, and learn from successes and failures. This adaptability ensures that the partnership remains relevant and practical, capable of meeting the changing needs of students and the community.

Finally, celebrating successes, no matter how small reinforces the partnership's value and energizes stakeholders to continue their efforts. Whether improving student attendance, launching a new community program, or recognizing volunteer contributions, taking the time to celebrate achievements fosters a positive and supportive atmosphere.

Creating a culture of partnership within schools and communities requires intentional efforts to build mutual respect, establish shared goals, enhance communication, empower stakeholders, build trust, adapt to change, and celebrate successes. This culture is not the end goal but an ongoing process that evolves with the partnership. It's the fertile ground from which innovative solutions to educational challenges can grow, where every student has the opportunity to succeed, and where communities become stronger and more cohesive. By committing to this collaborative journey, schools and communities can transform the educational landscape, making it more inclusive, dynamic, and reflective of our diverse world.

Long-term planning and goal setting

Long-term planning and goal setting are pivotal for the sustained success of school-community partnerships. These strategies ensure that collaborations are not just fleeting efforts but ingrained in the educational system and community fabric. Like a compass guiding a ship, long-term planning and clear goals provide direction, helping navigate challenges and ensuring that every action contributes to a larger vision.

The initial step in this journey involves establishing a shared vision that reflects the school's aspirations and the community's needs. This vision is the foundation for all future planning, uniting stakeholders around common objectives. Engaging a wide range of voices in creating this vision, from students and parents to teachers and community leaders, ensures it is comprehensive and inclusive.

Once the vision is set, the next stage is to define specific, measurable, achievable, relevant, and time-bound (SMART) goals. These objectives simplify tracking development and making necessary modifications by converting the overarching vision into concrete actions. For instance, if the shared vision focuses on improving student literacy, a corresponding SMART goal could be to increase the reading levels of 80% of students by one grade level within the next academic year.

Effective long-term planning also requires assessing the resources available and those that need to be acquired. This might include financial resources, human capital, or physical spaces. Understanding these resources helps outline a realistic plan that considers the school's and community's capabilities and limitations.

Collaboration is critical in the planning process. Schools and communities should work together to identify priorities, divide responsibilities, and decide on the best strategies to achieve their goals. This collaborative approach ensures that initiatives are well-supported and that efforts are synergized, avoiding duplication and maximizing impact.

Flexibility and adaptability are critical components of long-term planning. The educational landscape and community needs can change rapidly, and plans must be able to accommodate these shifts. Regular reviews of goals and strategies on an annual or bi-annual basis allow for timely adjustments in response to new challenges or opportunities.

Monitoring and evaluation are integral to long-term planning. They provide a framework for assessing the effectiveness of partnership activities and the progress toward goals. This could involve collecting data on student achievement, participation rates in partnership programs, or the impact of community services on families. These insights not only inform future planning but also help to maintain accountability and transparency among all stakeholders.

Finally, it is essential to communicate the long-term plan and its goals to all stakeholders. Regular updates, whether through newsletters, community meetings, or social media, keep the community informed and engaged. Celebrating milestones and acknowledging contributions fosters a sense of accomplishment and motivates continued involvement.

Long-term planning and goal setting are crucial for the vitality and effectiveness of school-community partnerships. By establishing a shared vision, defining clear goals, assessing resources, collaborating closely, remaining flexible, monitoring progress, and communicating effectively, schools and communities can create a sustainable partnership that enriches the educational experience and strengthens the community fabric. This strategic approach ensures that partnerships are not merely reactive but are proactive forces for positive change, guiding students toward success and communities toward a brighter future.

Evaluating partnership effectiveness and impact

Evaluating the effectiveness and impact of school-community partnerships is essential for understanding their value and guiding future improvements. This evaluation process systematically assesses how the partnership activities contribute to educational goals and community well-being. By measuring the outcomes, stakeholders can determine whether the partnership meets its objectives and where adjustments may be needed.

Developing Evaluation Criteria

The first step in evaluating partnership effectiveness is establishing clear criteria aligning with the partnership's goals. These criteria could range from academic improvements, such as student test scores or graduation rates, to broader community impacts, such as enhanced family engagement or improved access to community services for students and families. Establishing what success looks like from the outset ensures that all stakeholders have a common understanding of the partnership's objectives.

Collecting Data

Practical evaluation relies on the collection of relevant and reliable data. This might include quantitative data, such as attendance records, academic performance indicators, survey results, and qualitative data from interviews, focus groups, and case studies. Engaging a mix of data sources provides:

- A comprehensive view of the partnership's impact.
- Capturing the tangible outcomes and the more nuanced effects on school culture.
- Student well-being.
- Community cohesion.

Involving Stakeholders in the Evaluation Process

It is crucial to involve many stakeholders in the evaluation process. This includes students, parents, teachers, community partners, and possibly external evaluators. Their diverse perspectives enrich the evaluation, ensuring it considers the partnership's impact from multiple angles. Additionally, involving stakeholders in the evaluation process helps to foster a sense of ownership and accountability, strengthening the commitment to the partnership's success.

Analyzing and Interpreting Data

Once data is collected, the next step is to analyze and interpret the findings. This analysis should seek to answer critical questions: Are the partnership's goals being met? What aspects of the partnership are most effective? Where are these areas for improvement? Analyzing trends over time can also provide insights into the partnership's long-term impact and sustainability.

Reporting Findings

Communicating the evaluation findings is as important as the evaluation itself. Transparently sharing successes, challenges, and lessons learned helps build stakeholder trust and informs decision-making. Reports should be accessible and engaging, highlighting key outcomes and offering recommendations for future action. Publicizing these findings can also demonstrate the value of the partnership to the broader community and potential funders.

Using Evaluation to Guide Improvement

The ultimate goal of evaluating partnership effectiveness is to guide continuous improvement. Stakeholders should use the evaluation findings to celebrate achievements, address challenges, and refine strategies. This might involve expanding successful initiatives, rethinking less effective ones, or identifying new opportunities for collaboration. Regular evaluation ensures that the partnership remains responsive to the evolving needs of students and the community.

Fostering a Culture of Continuous Learning

It is essential to create a culture of ongoing learning and development. Encouraging open dialogue about what is working and what isn't and being willing to make evidence-based adjustments is critical to the partnership's long-term success. This culture of reflection and adaptability can help sustain the partnership through changes in leadership, funding, and community needs.

Evaluating the effectiveness and impact of school-community partnerships is a dynamic and collaborative process that enhances accountability, informs decision-making, and fosters continuous improvement. Through careful planning, stakeholder involvement, data-driven analysis, and transparent communication, schools and communities can ensure their partnerships meet current objectives and adapt and grow to meet future challenges. This ongoing evaluation process is essential for maintaining vibrant, effective partnerships that enrich the educational landscape and strengthen community ties.

Continuous improvement and adaptation

Continuous improvement and adaptation are critical principles for the growth and sustainability of school-community partnerships. Like a tree that adjusts its growth to the changing seasons, these partnerships must evolve to meet new challenges and opportunities. This dynamic process ensures that collaborations remain relevant, impactful, and responsive to the needs of students, schools, and the wider community.

Embracing a Mindset of Growth

The journey starts with embracing a mindset of growth and learning. Recognizing that there is always room for enhancement encourages stakeholders to seek new ideas, learn from experiences, and remain open to change. This mindset fosters an environment where feedback is welcomed, successes are built upon, and setbacks are viewed as opportunities for learning.

Setting the Stage for Continuous Learning

Creating a culture of continuous improvement requires intentional strategies. It involves regular reflection on practices, outcomes, and processes. Stakeholders should regularly convene to review what's working and what isn't, drawing on data and feedback from various sources. These reflective practices should be ingrained in the partnership's operations, with dedicated times for evaluation and planning for the future.

Leveraging Data for Informed Decision-Making

Data plays a crucial role in this process. By systematically collecting and analyzing data related to the partnership's goals, stakeholders can make informed decisions about where to focus their efforts. This might include academic performance data, attendance rates, community survey responses, or anecdotal evidence from students and families. Data highlights areas for improvement and helps identify successful strategies that can be expanded or replicated.

Adapting to Changing Needs and Contexts

The needs of students and communities, as well as the broader societal context, are constantly evolving. Partnerships that can adjust to these changes are considered adequate. This may involve shifting focus areas, introducing new programs, or altering collaboration methods. Flexibility and responsiveness are essential, allowing the partnership to remain aligned with its core mission while being agile enough to respond to new challenges and opportunities.

Fostering Collaboration and Shared Leadership

Collaboration is at the heart of continuous improvement. Partnerships can access a vast range of viewpoints, abilities, and expertise by incorporating a variety of stakeholders in the decision-making procedure. Shared leadership models can further enhance this collaborative approach, where responsibilities and leadership roles are distributed among school and community members. This ensures that improvement efforts are informed by those most closely connected to the partnership's work.

Investing in Professional Development and Capacity Building

Building the capacity of all stakeholders to contribute to the partnership's goals is essential for continuous improvement. This might involve professional development opportunities for teachers and school staff, training for community partners, or workshops for parents and families. Investing in developing skills and knowledge ensures that everyone involved has the tools to contribute to the partnership's success effectively.

Celebrating Successes and Learning from Failures

Recognizing and celebrating successes reinforces the value of the partnership and motivates continued engagement. At the same time, openly discussing and learning from failures or challenges can lead to valuable insights and innovation. Creating a safe space for sharing successes and setbacks encourages a culture of honesty and continuous learning.

Incorporating Innovation and Experimentation

Continuous improvement often requires innovation and experimentation. Trying new approaches, piloting programs, or adopting new technologies can lead to breakthroughs in how partnerships support student learning and community engagement. While only some innovations will be successful, fostering an environment where experimentation is encouraged can lead to significant advancements.

Continuous improvement and adaptation are not just strategies but fundamental principles that guide the development and sustainability of school-community partnerships. These partnerships can thrive by embracing a growth mindset, leveraging data, adapting to change, and fostering collaboration, investing in capacity building, celebrating successes, and incorporating innovation. This strategy leaves a long-lasting legacy of growth and progress by ensuring that school-community interactions stay dynamic, influential, and adaptable to the changing demands of students and communities.

CHAPTER 8

In the evolving education landscape, emerging trends in school-community partnerships reflect a growing recognition of their potential to enrich student learning and strengthen community ties. These partnerships are increasingly seen as vital resources for addressing complex educational challenges and preparing students for a rapidly changing world. Several key trends have emerged as schools and communities navigate these collaborations, signaling shifts in how these partnerships are formed, function, and contribute to educational and community development.

Technology Integration and Digital Collaboration

The integration of technology has dramatically transformed school-community partnerships. Digital platforms facilitate communication and collaboration between schools, families, and community members. Online tools and social media allow the sharing of information, resources, and learning opportunities beyond the physical classroom. This trend extends the reach of educational programs. It enables innovative forms of engagement, such as virtual volunteering, online mentorship, and digital community service projects, making participation more accessible to a broader audience.

Focus on Holistic Education

There's an increasing emphasis on partnerships that support not just academic achievement but the holistic development of students. Schools collaborate with community organizations to provide students with experiences promoting social-emotional learning, physical well-being, and life skills. These collaborations, from community sports programs and arts initiatives to mental health resources and nutrition education, ensure that students are healthy, engaged, and well-rounded.

Community-Based Learning Opportunities

Another trend is the growing utilization of the community as a vibrant classroom. Schools partner with local businesses, cultural institutions, and environmental organizations to offer real-world learning experiences. These opportunities expose students to potential career paths, practical applications of academic knowledge, and civic engagement. Such experiences enhance education's relevance and help students develop a deeper connection to their community.

Equity and Inclusion

Equity and inclusion have become central themes in school-community partnerships. There's a concerted effort to ensure these collaborations address educational disparities and provide equitable opportunities for all students. Partnerships are increasingly focused on reaching underserved populations, with programs designed to close the achievement gap, increase access to enrichment activities, and support families in navigating educational challenges. This trend reflects a broader commitment to creating more inclusive, supportive academic environments.

Sustainability and Environmental Education

With schools collaborating with community organizations to advance environmental education and sustainable practices, sustainability has become a significant concern. These partnerships involve initiatives like school gardens, recycling programs, and conservation projects, which teach students about environmental stewardship while contributing to the community's sustainability goals. This trend underscores the importance of preparing students to be responsible global citizens equipped to address environmental challenges.

Professional Development and Community Expertise

There's a growing recognition of the value of community expertise in professional development for educators. Schools are tapping into the wealth of knowledge within their communities to provide teachers with unique learning opportunities. Whether local engineers offer workshops on STEM subjects or artists lead professional development in creative pedagogies, these collaborations enrich the teaching experience and enhance educational quality.

Parent and Family Engagement

There has been a surge in the development of more focused approaches by communities and schools to include families in the educational process to increase parent and family participation. Since families are children's first instructors, partnerships provide parents with the knowledge, skills, and self-assurance they need to assist their kids' learning at home and in the community. This trend emphasizes the crucial role of families in education and seeks to strengthen the home-school connection.

Finally, the ability to be responsive and adaptive has become a hallmark of successful school-community partnerships. In an ever-changing social and economic landscape, these collaborations are designed to be flexible, allowing them to respond to emerging needs and opportunities quickly. This agility ensures that partnerships can continue to provide valuable support to students and communities, even in the face of challenges.

The emerging trends in school-community partnerships highlight a shift towards more innovative, inclusive, and holistic educational approaches. By leveraging technology, focusing on the whole child, utilizing community resources, prioritizing equity, promoting sustainability, tapping into local expertise, engaging families, and remaining adaptable, these collaborations set the stage for a future where education is a shared responsibility and a source of community strength. These trends not only enrich the educational experience for students but also foster a sense of unity and purpose within communities, building a foundation for collective success.

Leveraging technology for enhanced collaboration

Leveraging technology for enhanced collaboration in school-community partnerships marks a significant evolution in how these alliances operate, connect, and deliver results. The digital age has ushered in tools and platforms that break down traditional barriers, facilitating an unimaginable level of interaction and engagement. This transformation is not just about adopting new gadgets; it's about harnessing the power of technology to create more dynamic, inclusive, and impactful partnerships.

The cornerstone of leveraging technology in these collaborations is improved communication. Digital platforms like school websites, social media, and email newsletters have become essential channels for sharing information and celebrating successes. They allow schools to reach a broader audience, including families, community members, and local organizations, keeping everyone informed and engaged. Moreover, these platforms offer opportunities for two-way communication, enabling stakeholders to ask questions, provide feedback, and contribute ideas, fostering a more interactive and participatory relationship.

Virtual meeting technology has also revolutionized how meetings and workshops are conducted. Tools such as video conferencing software enable stakeholders from different locations to come together, discuss ideas, and make decisions without the need for physical travel. This accessibility ensures that more voices may be heard and included in the partnership's activities, which is especially helpful for working parents, distant community members, and partners with limited time.

Collaborative platforms and project management tools offer another layer of technological enhancement. These platforms allow for real-time collaboration on projects, sharing of resources, and tracking of progress. Whether planning a community event, co-developing curriculum materials, or organizing volunteer schedules, these tools streamline coordination and ensure everyone is on the same page. They promote transparency, accountability, and efficiency, which are critical to successful partnerships.

Technology also opens up new avenues for learning and engagement. Educational apps and online learning platforms provide students access to many resources and experiences beyond the classroom. Partnerships can leverage these tools to offer students online tutoring, virtual field trips, and access to online libraries and museums. This enriches the learning experience and ensures that educational opportunities are more equitable and accessible to all students, regardless of their geographical location or socio-economic status.

Social media plays a unique role in leveraging technology for collaboration. Schools and community organizations can use social media platforms to share stories, highlight achievements, and promote events. These platforms can also serve as powerful tools for rallying community support, crowdfunding for projects, or mobilizing volunteers. Schools can build a more robust, connected network of supporters and advocates by engaging with the community through social media.

Data analytics and feedback tools offer insights that can drive continuous partnership improvement. Surveys, polls, and analytics platforms provide valuable data on stakeholder satisfaction, program impact, and areas for growth. By regularly collecting and analyzing this data, partnerships can adapt their strategies to meet the community's needs better and enhance the effectiveness of their collaboration.

Integrating technology into school-community partnerships is crucial to ensuring accessibility and inclusivity. This means considering the digital divide and working to provide access to technology for all stakeholders. Community groups and schools may offer digital literacy training, give underprivileged families access to gadgets or the Internet, and ensure that online information is accessible to those with impairments. By addressing these challenges, partnerships can ensure that the benefits of technology are equitably shared.

Finally, leveraging technology requires a commitment to digital citizenship and safety. As partnerships increasingly rely on digital platforms, educating students, families, and community members about responsible online behavior, privacy, and data protection is essential. Creating a culture of digital citizenship ensures that technology is used in a way that is respectful, secure, and aligned with the partnership's values.

Leveraging technology for enhanced collaboration in school-community partnerships represents a significant shift towards more dynamic, accessible, and impactful collaborations. By improving communication, facilitating virtual participation, enabling real-time collaboration, enriching learning opportunities, engaging the broader community through social media, utilizing data for improvement, ensuring accessibility, and promoting digital citizenship, technology can transform these partnerships. As schools and communities navigate this digital landscape, they must focus on using technology for innovation and as a tool to deepen connections, broaden participation, and achieve shared goals, ultimately enriching the educational experience and strengthening the community fabric.

Exploring new models of cultural brokerage

Exploring new models of cultural brokerage within school-community partnerships offers fresh perspectives on bridging the gaps between diverse cultural backgrounds and the education system. As our societies become increasingly multicultural, the role of cultural brokers—individuals or entities facilitating understanding and communication between different cultural groups—has never been more critical. These new models are about translating languages and cultures, values, and expectations to foster a more inclusive and effective educational environment.

One innovative model of cultural brokerage involves integrating cultural competence training within schools. This technique will help teachers and other school staff better understand, relate to, and collaborate with kids and families from various cultural backgrounds. Training programs cover multiple aspects, including cultural awareness, anti-bias education, and strategies for inclusive communication. By embedding cultural competence into the fabric of the educational system, schools become proactive brokers of cultural understanding, creating a learning environment where all students feel valued and understood.

Another model focuses on community liaison officers or cultural liaisons who act as bridges between the school and its diverse communities. These individuals come from within the community and deeply understand its cultural nuances. They work within schools to provide culturally relevant family engagement programs, facilitate communication between families and educators, and support students struggling with cultural adaptation. This model highly values personal relationships and trust-building, recognizing that effective cultural brokerage is often rooted in genuine connections and empathy.

Digital networks have also made new kinds of cultural brokerage possible. Online resources and social media can serve as dynamic cultural exchange and education spaces. Schools can leverage these platforms to share cultural stories, celebrate diverse traditions, and provide families with multilingual resources. Additionally, virtual meeting spaces can facilitate dialogue and collaboration among educators, families, and community members, overcoming geographical barriers and enabling broader participation in the school community.

Collaborative networks that bring together various stakeholders—schools, families, community organizations, and cultural institutions—represent another model of cultural brokerage. These networks operate on the principle of collective impact, where all parties work together towards shared goals, such as improving educational outcomes for culturally diverse students or enhancing cultural understanding within the community. By pooling resources, knowledge, and expertise, these networks can implement comprehensive programs and initiatives that address the multifaceted needs of students and their families.

Peer mentoring programs within schools offer a peer-to-peer model of cultural brokerage. Older students or those who are more acculturated serve as mentors to younger students or newcomers, guiding them through the social and academic landscape of the school. These programs support the mentees' adaptation and learning and foster leadership skills and cultural pride among the mentors. Peer mentoring emphasizes the value of shared experiences and mutual support, highlighting students' role in cultural brokerage.

Incorporating cultural storytelling and art into the curriculum is a powerful model for cultural brokerage. Through stories, music, dance, and visual arts, students can explore and express their cultural identities, share them with their peers, and learn about other cultures meaningfully. This approach enhances cultural understanding and enriches the educational experience for all students by integrating diverse perspectives and modes of learning.

Community-based learning experiences that connect students with their local communities offer practical opportunities for cultural brokerage. These experiences, which can include service projects to internships with local companies or cultural organizations, let students apply their academic knowledge to real-world situations and gain a deeper appreciation for their community's rich cultural variety. Schools facilitate these experiences, ensuring they align with curricular goals and support students' artistic and personal development.

Exploring new models of cultural brokerage in school-community partnerships is essential for addressing the challenges and opportunities our increasingly diverse societies present. Through cultural competence training, liaison officers, digital platforms, collaborative networks, peer mentoring, artistic storytelling, or community-based learning, these models offer innovative ways to enhance cultural understanding and integration. By adopting and adapting these models, schools and communities can work together to create educational environments that respect, celebrate, and leverage cultural diversity to benefit all students.

Recommendations for policymakers, educators, and community leaders

Strengthening school-community partnerships and leveraging the unique role of cultural brokers require policymakers, educators, and community leaders to work collaboratively to create more inclusive, responsive, and effective educational environments. The following recommendations are designed to guide these stakeholders in enhancing their collaborative efforts and ensuring that every student benefits from a supportive and enriching academic experience.

For Policymakers

Prioritize Funding: Allocate resources for programs promoting school-community engagement and cultural brokerage. This includes funding for educators' professional development in cultural competence and support for initiatives that facilitate parental involvement, particularly for English Language Learner (ELL) families and other marginalized groups.

Develop Inclusive Policies: Craft policies that encourage schools to adopt culturally responsive pedagogies and curricula. Policies should also support technology integration in ways that bridge rather than widen the digital divide, ensuring equitable access to digital learning resources.

Encourage Community Collaboration: Incentivize partnerships between schools and local organizations, businesses, and cultural institutions. Such collaborations can provide students with a wealth of resources, knowledge, and opportunities, enhancing their educational experience beyond the classroom.

For Educators

Cultivate Cultural Competence: Take part in continuing professional development to increase your awareness of and respect for the cultural variety within the student body. This understanding is essential to fostering a climate in the classroom where each kid feels respected and understood.

Implement Inclusive Practices: Adopt teaching methods and curricular materials that reflect students' cultural backgrounds and experiences. Please encourage students to share their cultural perspectives and integrate these insights into learning.

Foster Open Communication: Develop clear, effective communication channels with families and community members. Use technology and other tools to guarantee that everyone can communicate, regardless of language obstacles.

For Community Leaders

Act as Cultural Brokers: Take an active role in bridging the cultural and linguistic gaps between schools and the communities they serve. Offer your knowledge, networks, and resources to facilitate understanding and collaboration.

Support Educational Initiatives: Engage with local schools to understand their needs and how your organization or business can enhance students' educational experience. Whether through volunteering, mentorship programs, or resource sharing, your involvement can make a significant difference.

Promote Community Engagement: Encourage community members to participate in school activities and decision-making processes. A community that is actively involved in its schools fosters a sense of shared responsibility and commitment to the success of its students.

By implementing these suggestions, educators, legislators, and community leaders may collaborate to create more robust and dynamic alliances that enhance student learning and equip them to be involved, active citizens of a multicultural and international society.

CHAPTER 9

The digital transformation in education and community engagement represents a profound shift in how teaching, learning, and collaboration are approached. This transformation is not merely about adopting new technologies; it's about rethinking the essence of education and community interaction in the digital age. It involves leveraging digital tools to create more accessible, engaging, and effective educational experiences and foster deeper community connections.

At the heart of this transformation is integrating digital technology into all areas of education. This includes utilizing online learning environments, which remove the limitations of conventional classroom walls by enabling students to access course content and resources at any time, from any location. These platforms support various learning activities, from interactive lessons and video lectures to online discussions and assessments, catering to diverse learning styles and needs.

Digital transformation also encompasses educational apps and games that make learning more interactive and fun. These resources raise students' motivation and engagement, making complex subjects more approachable and entertaining. Furthermore, virtual and augmented reality technologies have begun to enter the educational sphere, offering immersive experiences that can bring historical events to life, simulate scientific experiments, or explore the natural world in unprecedented ways.

Digital transformation, another critical factor, makes personalized learning possible. Adaptive learning technology allows educational materials to be customized to fit each student's unique requirements and learning styles. This tailored strategy ultimately results in better learning results, guaranteeing that students receive the encouragement and challenges they need to advance.

The role of digital technology in fostering community engagement within the educational context has also expanded. Students, teachers, and community members may exchange information, discuss problems, and collaborate on projects using social media and online forums. These digital communities can support a sense of belonging and collective purpose, extending the reach and impact of educational initiatives.

Digital transformation has also led to the development of new models of teacher professional development. Online courses, webinars, and collaborative learning communities enable educators to update their skills and share best practices continuously. Teachers must continue to improve professionally to successfully incorporate digital technologies into their lessons and meet the difficulties of the digital era.

Data analytics and digital assessment tools offer another advantage: They provide educators valuable insights into student learning and engagement. By examining data from digital learning activities, teachers may spot patterns, track advancement, and make wise judgments to enhance their methods of instruction. This data-driven approach supports a more responsive and effective educational system.

Moreover, the digital transformation in education opens up opportunities for greater community involvement. Through online platforms, community members can contribute to educational content, participate in school governance, or mentor students. This collaboration can enrich the academic experience with real-world perspectives and expertise, bridging the gap between schools and the broader community.

However, the digital transformation also presents challenges. Issues such as the digital divide, where access to technology and the internet are not equally available to all students, can exacerbate educational inequalities. There's also the need for digital literacy among students, educators, and community members to ensure that digital tools are used effectively and responsibly. Collaboratively addressing these concerns, educators, policymakers, and community leaders must ensure everyone can reap the benefits of the digital shift.

The digital transformation in education and community engagement is reshaping the landscape of learning and collaboration. By harnessing the power of digital technology, educational experiences can become more accessible, personalized, and engaging, while community connections are strengthened through new platforms for interaction and collaboration. As this transformation unfolds, it's imperative to navigate its challenges thoughtfully, ensuring that the digital future of education is inclusive, equitable, and beneficial for all community members.

Social media, applications, and platforms are used effectively to form partnerships

In today's digital era, the effective use of social media, apps, and platforms has become indispensable in fostering and strengthening partnerships, especially within education and community engagement. These digital tools offer unprecedented opportunities to connect, communicate, and collaborate, breaking traditional barriers and opening new partnership-building avenues.

Social Media for Community Engagement

The way local organizations and educational institutions connect and communicate with their audiences has drastically changed due to social media sites like Facebook, Instagram, and Twitter. By creating dedicated social media pages, schools can share news, achievements, and events with the community in real time, fostering a sense of pride and belonging among students, parents, and community members. Social media also allows for two-way communication, where feedback and ideas can be shared, creating a dynamic and interactive relationship between schools and their communities.

One effective technique is using social media to hold live Q&A sessions or discussions with educators, school administrators, or community partners. These events can address community concerns, highlight partnership initiatives, or discuss educational topics, engaging a broad audience and fostering transparency and trust. Social media campaigns can also rally support for community projects, celebrate successes, or promote volunteer opportunities, mobilizing community action and support.

Apps for Collaboration and Communication

Various apps have also emerged as powerful tools for enhancing collaboration and communication among partnership stakeholders. Messaging apps like WhatsApp and collaboration platforms like Slack or Microsoft Teams enable efficient and direct communication between teachers, parents, and community partners. These tools facilitate quick updates, share resources, and coordinate activities without the delays of traditional communication methods.

Educational apps and platforms, such as Google Classroom, Schoology, or Edmodo, provide shared spaces for learning and collaboration. Teachers can post assignments, share educational resources, and provide feedback, while parents and students can access learning materials and track progress. These platforms can also involve community partners in the educational process, allowing them to contribute resources, guest lectures, or project-based learning opportunities.

Using Platforms for Resource Sharing and Crowdsourcing

Digital platforms can also be utilized for resource sharing and crowdsourcing, leveraging the community's collective knowledge, skills, and resources. Sites like DonorsChoose or GoFundMe enable schools to raise funds for projects, equipment, or programs, tapping into the community's generosity and beyond. Similarly, platforms such as Trello or Padlet can organize and share resources, plan events, or collaborate on projects, making it easier for multiple stakeholders to contribute and stay informed.

Another innovative application of digital platforms is the creation of virtual community boards or forums where community members can post needs, offers, and opportunities. This open exchange can lead to unexpected partnerships and collaborations as resources and needs are matched dynamically and organically.

Engaging Content to Capture Attention

To maximize the impact of social media, apps, and platforms, it's crucial to produce engaging and relevant content. This might include videos showcasing community partnership projects, infographics highlighting achievements or goals, or stories from students, teachers, and community members that personalize the partnership experience. Engaging content captures Attention and fosters emotional connections, making stakeholders more likely to participate actively and support the partnership.

Training and Guidelines for Effective Use

For social media, apps, and platforms to be used effectively, stakeholders need appropriate training and guidelines. This ensures that digital tools are used responsibly and productively, with a clear understanding of privacy, security, and etiquette. Training sessions for teachers, parents, and community partners can cover topics such as digital communication best practices, content creation, and data protection, ensuring that everyone is equipped to contribute positively to the digital partnership ecosystem.

Using social media, apps, and platforms effectively holds immense potential for building and enhancing partnerships in education and community engagement. These digital tools can create more vibrant, inclusive, and impactful partnerships by fostering transparent communication, facilitating collaboration, and engaging the wider community. However, success in this digital endeavor requires thoughtful planning, ongoing training, and a commitment to creating meaningful and engaging content that resonates with all stakeholders. As we navigate the digital age, harnessing these tools for partnership-building will be vital to building more robust, more connected communities.

Case Studies on successful technology integration in school-community Initiatives

In education, technology integration has opened doors to innovative school-community initiatives, demonstrating the transformative power of digital tools in enhancing learning and fostering community engagement. Exploring case studies of successful technology integration offers insights and inspiration for schools looking to harness the benefits of digital advancements.

Case Study 1: Virtual Reality Environmental Science Program

In a mid-sized city, a high school partnered with a local environmental organization to create a virtual reality (VR) program for environmental science education. The program utilized VR headsets to immerse students in diverse ecosystems, from coral reefs to rainforests, providing an up-close look at habitats, biodiversity, and environmental challenges. This initiative enriched the curriculum with cutting-edge technology and fostered a deeper understanding of and engagement with environmental issues among students. The program's success led to its expansion, with the school hosting community events where parents and residents could experience the VR journeys, strengthening community awareness and support for environmental conservation.

Case Study 2: Community Coding Workshops

Due to limited resources, a rural community faced challenges in providing students with access to STEM (Science, Technology, Engineering, and Mathematics) education. In response, a local school district collaborated with a technology company to launch a series of coding workshops for students and community members. These workshops, held at the school's computer lab, were facilitated by professionals from the technology company and aimed to develop coding skills, critical thinking, and problem-solving abilities. The initiative provided valuable learning opportunities and sparked interest in STEM careers among students. Additionally, involving community members, the workshops fostered a culture of lifelong learning and showcased the potential for technology to bridge educational gaps.

Case Study 3: Digital Literacy Campaign

Recognizing the importance of digital literacy in today's world, a school partnered with a community library to launch a digital literacy campaign. The campaign offered workshops and resources on navigating the internet safely, using social media responsibly, and leveraging online tools for learning and productivity. The initiative targeted students, parents, and elderly community members, aiming to improve digital skills across generations. Through collaboration, the school and library were able to reach a broad audience, promoting digital literacy as a foundational skill for participation in the digital age. The campaign also facilitated intergenerational learning, with students assisting older community members and strengthening community bonds through shared learning experiences.

Case Study 4: Online Community Art Exhibition

An elementary school in a culturally diverse neighborhood initiated an online community art exhibition to celebrate the artistic talents of students and community members. Using a digital platform, participants submitted artworks inspired by their cultural heritage, which were then showcased in a virtual gallery. The initiative provided a space for artistic expression and promoted cultural understanding and appreciation within the community. The online format enabled broader participation, including from relatives living abroad, and the exhibition's success led to its establishment as an annual event, highlighting the role of technology in celebrating diversity and fostering community pride.

Case Study 5: Telehealth Mental Wellness Program

A school district and a nearby health facility collaborated to create a telehealth mental wellness program in response to rising student mental health concerns. The program provided students remote access to counseling and mental health resources using secure video conferencing tools. This initiative addressed barriers to accessing mental health services, such as stigma and transportation, and offered a flexible option for students and families. By integrating technology into mental health support, the school and clinic were able to provide timely, confidential assistance, demonstrating the potential of digital solutions in addressing critical community needs.

These case studies highlight how integrating technology into education may improve student performance and encourage community involvement. From immersive learning experiences and skill-building workshops to campaigns promoting digital literacy and cultural expression, technology catalyzes innovative initiatives that bring schools and communities closer together. By exploring and adopting successful models of technology integration, schools can unlock new possibilities for collaboration, learning, and community development, paving the way for a future where education is more accessible, engaging, and connected to the broader world.

Challenges and ethical considerations in digital engagement strategies

Navigating the digital landscape presents challenges and ethical considerations, especially regarding engagement strategies in education and community initiatives. While digital tools offer unprecedented opportunities for connection and learning, they also raise important questions about privacy, equity, and the responsible use of technology.

Privacy and Data Protection

Ensuring the privacy and safety of personal data is one of the biggest obstacles. Digital platforms gather enormous user data, including private information about pupils and neighbors. It is critical to safeguard sensitive data from breaches and unwanted access. Schools and organizations must adhere to strict data protection regulations, such as GDPR in Europe or FERPA in the United States, which govern personal information collection, storage, and use. Implementing robust security measures and educating users about privacy settings and data rights are essential to safeguarding privacy.

Equity and Access

The digital divide is another significant challenge. Despite the proliferation of digital devices and internet access, disparities persist, with some students and community members needing more resources to participate fully in digital initiatives. This gap can exacerbate existing inequalities, limiting opportunities for learning and engagement. Addressing this challenge requires concerted efforts to provide affordable devices, internet access, and digital literacy training to ensure that digital engagement strategies are inclusive and accessible to all.

Screen Time and Well-being

Particularly among young people, worries about excessive screen use and its effects on well-being are becoming more prevalent. Digital involvement may improve learning and connectedness, but finding a balance is essential to prevent negative consequences on one's physical or mental health. Strategies to mitigate these concerns include:

- Promoting digital wellness practices, such as setting limits on screen time.
- Encouraging breaks.
- Balancing digital activities with offline experiences.

Schools and community groups are essential in setting an example of good digital citizenship and sensibly offering advice on using the internet.

Misinformation and Cyberbullying

The spread of misinformation and the risk of cyberbullying are further challenges in the digital realm. Digital platforms can be conduits for false information and harmful behavior, impacting individuals and communities. Combating these issues requires a proactive approach, including educating users about critical thinking and digital literacy, implementing robust moderation policies, and supporting those affected by online harassment. A positive and respectful online culture is essential for safe and productive digital engagement.

Ethical Content Creation

Creating and sharing digital content also raises ethical considerations. Ensuring that content is accurate, respectful, and culturally sensitive is crucial. This involves vetting materials for bias, stereotypes, or inappropriate content and considering the diverse backgrounds and perspectives of the audience. Engaging with community members in content creation can help ensure that digital materials are inclusive and reflect community values.

Informed Consent

Consent should be informed, voluntary, and revocable, with clear communication about how the content will be used and who will have access to it. Respecting individuals' rights to privacy and control over personal information is fundamental to ethical digital engagement.

Sustainability

Finally, the sustainability of digital initiatives is an important consideration. This includes digital technology's environmental impact and digital programs' long-term viability. Ensuring that digital engagement strategies are environmentally responsible and have a clear plan for maintenance, updates, and support is essential for their success and sustainability.

While digital engagement strategies offer potent opportunities for enhancing education and community initiatives, they also present complex challenges and ethical considerations. Addressing these issues requires a thoughtful, inclusive approach that prioritizes privacy, equity, well-being, and responsible use of technology. By navigating these challenges ethically and proactively, schools and organizations can harness the benefits of digital engagement to create more connected, informed, and inclusive communities.

CHAPTER 10

In the collaborative landscape of school-community partnerships, data-driven decision-making stands as a beacon, guiding the way toward more effective, impactful, and sustainable collaborations. This approach, which emphasizes using data to inform and drive decisions, is pivotal for the success of partnerships to enhance educational outcomes and strengthen communities.

Enhancing Clarity and Direction

Data-driven decision-making brings clarity and direction to partnerships. Collecting and analyzing relevant data allows stakeholders to identify the most pressing needs, prioritize objectives, and set clear, measurable goals. This process eliminates guesswork, allowing schools and community organizations to focus their resources and efforts where needed most. Whether it's improving student literacy rates, increasing access to extracurricular activities, or addressing community health concerns, data provides a solid foundation for defining the partnership's direction.

Facilitating Targeted Interventions

Designing and implementing focused interventions is one of the most significant benefits of data-driven decision-making. With detailed data on student performance, community needs, and program outcomes, partnerships can develop initiatives tailored to the specific challenges and opportunities they face. Based on a thorough comprehension of the situation and the individuals intended for assistance, this accuracy guarantees that interventions have a higher chance of success. For instance, data may reveal that students from specific neighbourhoods struggle with math, leading to targeted tutoring programs.

Improving Accountability and Transparency

Data-driven decision-making also enhances accountability and transparency within partnerships. By setting goals based on data and regularly measuring progress against these goals, partnerships can demonstrate their impact on stakeholders, including funders, participants, and the broader community. By showing how resources are being spent efficiently and how the partnership is having an effect, this openness helps foster trust and confidence in the relationship. It also allows stakeholders to celebrate successes and learn from challenges, fostering a culture of transparency and continuous improvement.

Enabling Adaptability and Responsiveness

Adapting and responding to new information is crucial in today's rapidly changing world. Data-driven decision-making ensures that partnerships remain dynamic and responsive. By continually collecting and analyzing data, partnerships can identify emerging trends, such as shifts in community needs or student performance. This ongoing insight allows them to adjust their strategies and initiatives in real-time, ensuring they remain relevant and practical. For example, data might show that online learning platforms are not reaching all students equally, prompting a resource shift to address digital divide issues.

Strengthening Collaborations

Data-driven decision-making can also strengthen collaborations between schools and community organizations. When decisions are based on shared data and evidence, it's easier for all parties to align their efforts and work towards common goals. This shared focus fosters a strengthened partnership and collaboration, as stakeholders are united in pursuing data-informed objectives. Additionally, data can help identify potential new partners whose services or resources align with the partnership's goals, expanding the support network for students and communities.

Promoting Equity

Importantly, data-driven decision-making promotes equity in school-community partnerships. By disaggregating data by race, ethnicity, socioeconomic status, and other demographics, partnerships can identify and address disparities in outcomes. This focused approach ensures that interventions are designed to reach and support the most marginalized and underserved community members, helping to close gaps in opportunity and achievement.

Challenges to Overcome

However, embracing data-driven decision-making is challenging. Partnerships must navigate issues related to data collection, privacy, and capacity. Ensuring the ethical use of data, protecting individuals' privacy, and building the capacity to collect, analyze, and interpret data are all critical considerations. Overcoming these challenges requires a commitment to ethical standards, investments in training and technology, and, where possible, partnerships with research organizations or data experts.

The importance of data-driven decision-making in school-community partnerships must be considered. It provides a foundation for informed decision-making, enhances the effectiveness and efficiency of interventions, and ensures that efforts are equitable and responsive to community needs. By committing to a data-driven approach, schools and community organizations can deepen their impact, fostering educational success and community well-being in a transparent, accountable, and adaptable way to the needs of those they serve.

Overview of current research on cultural brokerage in education

Current research is gaining significant attention to the concept of cultural brokerage in education, shedding light on its critical role in fostering inclusive and effective learning environments. This body of research focuses on understanding how cultural brokers—individuals or entities facilitating understanding and collaboration across cultural divides—can enhance educational outcomes and support diverse student populations. As societies become increasingly multicultural, the need for cultural brokerage in schools has never been more apparent.

Central to the research on cultural brokerage is exploring its impact on student achievement and well-being. Studies have shown that when schools effectively engage in cultural brokerage, students from culturally and linguistically diverse backgrounds experience improved academic performance, higher levels of engagement, and more excellent emotional support. This is attributed to the cultural brokers' ability to navigate and bridge the gap between students' home and school cultures, ensuring that educational practices are culturally responsive and inclusive.

Another focal point of research is identifying effective practices for cultural brokerage in schools. This includes developing strategies for enhancing communication between schools and diverse communities, implementing culturally relevant pedagogy, and engaging families and community members in the educational process. Collaborating with community groups and utilizing their resources and experience to help students with their language and cultural needs is a common strategy for effective cultural brokerage.

The role of teachers and school staff as cultural brokers is also a key area of inquiry. Research emphasizes the importance of professional development in cultural competence as a foundational skill for educators. Training programs that focus on understanding cultural diversity, addressing biases, and developing strategies for inclusive education are shown to equip teachers with the necessary skills to act as effective cultural brokers.

Moreover, the research explores the challenges and barriers to effective cultural brokerage in schools. These challenges include language barriers, limited resources for implementing culturally responsive practices, and systemic biases that may exist within the educational system. Comprehending these difficulties is essential to creating focused interventions and policies encouraging cultural brokerage in education.

Emerging trends in the research on cultural brokerage include using technology to facilitate cross-cultural understanding and collaboration. Digital platforms and tools offer new opportunities for cultural exchange, language learning, and engagement with diverse educational content. These technologies can expand the reach of cultural brokerage efforts, making it easier to connect students, families, and educators across geographical and cultural boundaries.

The research also highlights the importance of measuring cultural brokerage's impact on educational outcomes. This involves developing indicators and assessment tools to evaluate the effectiveness of cultural brokerage practices in improving student learning, engagement, and well-being. Such evaluation is essential for refining practices and demonstrating the value of cultural brokerage in education.

Current research on cultural brokerage in education underscores its significance in creating inclusive, supportive, and effective learning environments for all students. By focusing on the impact of cultural brokerage, identifying effective practices, exploring the role of educators, addressing challenges, and measuring outcomes, this body of research provides valuable insights for schools, policymakers, and community organizations. As the cultural landscape of societies continues to evolve, the need for continued research and implementation of cultural brokerage in education remains paramount, offering a pathway to more equitable and responsive educational systems.

Analyzing gaps in the literature and opportunities for future research

While the existing literature on cultural brokerage in education has illuminated its significance and impact, noticeable gaps present opportunities for future research. Addressing these gaps is essential for deepening our understanding of how cultural brokerage can be optimized to support diverse student populations and enhance educational outcomes.

One notable gap is the need for more research on the long-term effects of cultural brokerage interventions in schools. While short-term benefits, such as improved student engagement and academic performance, have been documented, longitudinal studies that track the lasting impact of cultural brokerage on students' educational trajectories and well-being are needed. Understanding the long-term outcomes can provide valuable insights into the sustainability and efficacy of cultural brokerage practices.

Another area that requires further exploration is the role of digital technology in cultural brokerage. Although emerging research has begun to explore this dimension, there is a vast potential for investigating how online platforms, digital tools, and social media can effectively bridge cultural divides and enhance communication between schools, families, and communities. Future research could focus on identifying best practices for digital cultural brokerage and assessing the challenges and opportunities technology presents in this context.

The literature also needs a comprehensive analysis of the challenges and barriers to implementing cultural brokerage in schools, particularly in regions or contexts where resources are scarce. Future studies could examine the specific obstacles schools face in low-income areas or countries with limited access to cultural and linguistic resources. Identifying these challenges can inform the development of targeted strategies and interventions adaptable to different educational settings and resource constraints.

Moreover, there is a need for more research on the perspectives and experiences of students, families, and community members who are at the receiving end of cultural brokerage efforts. Understanding the experiences of those directly impacted by cultural brokerage can provide essential insights into how these initiatives can be improved to better meet the needs of diverse student populations, even though the perspectives of educators and school administrators have been relatively well-documented.

Additionally, comparative studies examining cultural brokerage practices across different educational systems and contexts still need to be included. Such research could reveal how cultural brokerage is adapted to various settings, providing a richer understanding of effective cultural brokerage's universal and context-specific aspects. This could also highlight innovative practices that could be adopted or adapted by other regions or countries.

Another area ripe for exploration is the impact of cultural brokerage on specific student outcomes, such as social-emotional learning, identity development, and resilience. While the academic benefits of cultural brokerage have been emphasized, its influence on students' personal growth and well-being needs to be more understood. Research in this area could contribute to a more holistic view of the benefits of cultural brokerage in education.

Finally, there is an opportunity for research focusing on the training and professional development of cultural brokers. Investigating the skills, knowledge, and competencies required for effective cultural brokerage and the best practices for training educators and community members in this role can guide schools and organizations looking to strengthen their cultural brokerage initiatives.

While the literature on cultural brokerage in education has provided valuable insights, significant gaps offer opportunities for future research. Addressing these gaps can deepen our understanding of cultural brokerage, identify best practices and challenges, and ultimately contribute to more effective and inclusive educational practices. The significance of this research cannot be emphasized as societies continue to diversify in terms of culture. It provides a way forward for educational institutions catering to every student's requirements.

Translating research findings into practice for educators and community leaders

Translating research findings into practice is essential for educators and community leaders aiming to enhance educational outcomes and strengthen community ties. This process involves taking insights from academic studies and applying them in real-world educational settings to improve teaching, learning, and collaboration. By bridging the gap between research and practice, educators and community leaders can implement evidence-based strategies that make a tangible difference in the lives of students and communities.

Understanding Research Findings

The first step in translating research into practice is to thoroughly understand the findings. Educators and community leaders should engage with research studies on education, cultural brokerage, community engagement, and other relevant topics. This might involve participating in professional development workshops, attending academic conferences, or collaborating with researchers. The goal is to understand the evidence supporting various educational practices and interventions deeply.

Identifying Relevant Insights

Only some research findings will be directly applicable to some educational context. Therefore, educators and community leaders must identify insights most relevant to their specific settings and challenges. This involves considering the cultural, economic, and social context of the school or community and determining which research findings offer the most potential for positive impact. Prioritizing research that aligns with the community's needs and values ensures that the efforts to translate research into practice are meaningful and effective.

Adapting Strategies to Local Contexts

Translating research into practice requires adapting research-based strategies to fit local contexts. This means taking general findings and tailoring them to the unique characteristics of the school or community. For example, a plan for enhancing parental engagement in one community might need to be modified to address language barriers in another. Educators and community leaders play a crucial role in this adaptation process, using their knowledge of the local context to ensure that interventions are culturally responsive and practically feasible.

Implementing Changes Gradually

Change is often most effective when implemented gradually and with careful planning. Educators and community leaders should start by piloting research-based interventions on a small scale, gathering participant feedback, and making necessary adjustments. This iterative approach allows for fine-tuning strategies to maximize effectiveness before broader implementation. It also helps build stakeholders' buy-in by demonstrating commitment to evidence-based improvement and responsiveness to community feedback.

Evaluating impact

Evaluating the impact of implemented changes is essential to ensuring that research is translated into practice and achieves desired outcomes. This might involve collecting data on student performance, engagement levels, or other relevant indicators before and after the intervention. Regular evaluation not only provides evidence of the effectiveness of research-based practices but also identifies areas for further improvement.

Sharing Successes and Challenges

Sharing the experiences of translating research into practice, including successes and challenges, is vital for the broader educational community. Educators and community leaders can contribute to professional networks, publish articles in educational newsletters or journals, or present at conferences to share their insights. This information sharing promotes a culture of ongoing learning and development in education and contributes to research around practical approaches.

Fostering Collaboration between Researchers and Practitioners

Finally, strengthening the collaboration between researchers and practitioners is critical to effectively translating research findings into practice. Collaboration can take many forms: it might involve cooperative research initiatives or input on research goals from practitioner advisory boards. Such partnerships ensure that research is grounded in the realities of educational practice and that findings are communicated in accessible and actionable ways.

Putting research results into practice is a dynamic process that calls for thorough literature comprehension, cautious local context adaptation, slow implementation, continuous assessment, and candid experience sharing. By engaging in this process, educators and community leaders can leverage evidence-based strategies to enhance education and strengthen community partnerships, ultimately leading to improved outcomes for students and communities.

CHAPTER 11

Comparative analysis of partnership models across different countries reveals a rich tapestry of approaches, each shaped by its unique cultural, social, and educational context. These models, ranging from community-led initiatives in rural settings to government-driven programs in urban areas, offer valuable insights into the diverse strategies for fostering collaboration between schools and their communities. Exploring these models highlights the universal importance of school-community partnerships and underscores the adaptability and creativity of these collaborations to meet local needs.

Nordic Model: Emphasis on Equality and Inclusivity

In countries like Finland and Sweden, partnership models are deeply rooted in equality and inclusivity. The Nordic approach to education emphasizes comprehensive support for students, integrating academic learning with social and emotional development. Schools work closely with various community organizations, including social services, health care providers, and cultural institutions, to create a supportive student ecosystem. This model is characterized by its holistic perspective on education, where the child's well-being is paramount, and partnerships aim to support this goal through a wide range of services and activities.

United States: Diverse and Decentralized Approaches

The United States presents a diverse landscape of partnership models, reflecting the country's decentralized education system. Partnerships vary significantly from one district to another, with initiatives often driven by local needs and resources. Examples include after-school programs collaborating with local businesses and non-profits, community service projects integrated into the curriculum, and parent engagement programs designed to strengthen the home-school connection. This diversity allows for innovation and experimentation, leading to unique partnership models tailored to each community's challenges and opportunities.

Japan: Community Involvement in Moral and Civic Education

In Japan, school-community partnerships often focus on moral and civic education, with the community playing a significant role in teaching students about cultural traditions, social responsibilities, and civic duties. Local festivals, artistic workshops, and community service activities are common platforms for collaboration, allowing students to learn from and contribute to their communities. This model highlights the importance of cultural heritage and community values in education, with partnerships to nurture well-rounded individuals deeply connected to their community and culture.

Brazil: Bridging Educational Gaps in Marginalized Communities

In Brazil, partnerships between schools and communities are frequently driven by the need to address educational disparities and promote social justice. Many initiatives focus on providing access to quality education for students in marginalized communities, often involving collaborations with non-governmental organizations, local businesses, and international agencies. These partnerships may offer supplementary educational programs, vocational training, and health and nutrition services to remove barriers to education and empower students and their families. The Brazilian model underscores the potential of school-community partnerships to drive social change and promote equity in education.

India: Leveraging Technology for Rural Education

India offers an example of how technology can be leveraged to enhance school-community partnerships, especially in rural areas. Initiatives such as digital learning centers and mobile education vans bring educational resources to remote communities, breaking down geographical barriers to education. Partnerships with tech companies and non-profits are crucial in these initiatives, providing the necessary technology, content, and training to make digital education accessible. This model demonstrates the power of technology to extend the reach of educational partnerships and create new opportunities for learning in underserved areas.

Comparing these models from different countries reveals a common thread: recognizing the critical role that school-community partnerships play in enriching education and supporting students. Despite the diversity in approaches, these models are committed to leveraging local resources, knowledge, and expertise to enhance the educational experience. Through an analysis of these diverse methodologies, educators and policymakers may get valuable perspectives about the capacity of partnerships to adjust to local circumstances, address the distinct requirements of students and communities, and support the worldwide endeavor of providing high-quality education to all.

Lessons learned from international case studies on cultural brokerage

International case studies on cultural brokerage in education provide valuable insights and lessons on effectively bridging cultural gaps within diverse school communities. These studies, ranging from localized initiatives to national programs, underscore the importance of cultural understanding, empathy, and communication in fostering inclusive learning environments. Here are some critical lessons learned from these global experiences.

Embrace Cultural Diversity as an Asset

One of the foremost lessons is to view cultural diversity not as a challenge to overcome but as a valuable asset to embrace. Schools that successfully integrate cultural brokerage recognize the richness diverse perspectives bring to the educational experience. These institutions leverage their students' and communities' varied cultural backgrounds to enhance the curriculum, create more engaging learning experiences, and promote mutual understanding among students from different backgrounds.

Invest in Building Cultural Competence

Another critical lesson is investing in cultural competence for educators and school leaders. Professional development programs that focus on cultural awareness, sensitivity, and communication skills are essential. Educators equipped with these skills are better prepared to act as effective cultural brokers, navigating cultural nuances with respect and understanding and creating a classroom atmosphere where all students feel valued and included.

Foster Open and Inclusive Communication

Effective cultural brokerage relies on open and inclusive communication channels that allow all community members' voices to be heard. Schools that excel in this area create multiple avenues for dialogue, including parent-teacher meetings in various languages, community forums, and digital platforms that accommodate different communication preferences. Encouraging active participation from the entire school community ensures that diverse perspectives are considered in decision-making processes.

Collaborate with Community and Cultural Organizations

Partnering with local community and cultural organizations can significantly enhance a school's cultural brokerage efforts. These organizations often have deep insights into the community's cultural needs and assets. By collaborating, schools can access additional resources, expertise, and support for cultural events, language programs, and family engagement initiatives. These partnerships enrich the school's programs and strengthen ties between the school and its surrounding community.

Prioritize Empathy and Relationship Building

Effective cultural brokerage centers on empathy and the capacity to forge deep connections across cultural barriers. Case studies highlight the importance of empathy in understanding the experiences and challenges of culturally diverse students and their families. Schools prioritizing relationship building tend to create more supportive and trusting environments where students and families feel comfortable sharing their cultural identities and experiences.

Adapt and Be Flexible

The dynamic nature of cultural identities and community demographics requires schools to be adaptable and flexible in their cultural brokerage strategies. What works in one context may not be effective in another. Successful schools continuously assess the needs of their students and communities, are open to change, and are willing to innovate their approaches to cultural brokerage.

Evaluate and Reflect on Practices

Regular evaluation and reflection are crucial for sustaining and improving cultural brokerage efforts. Schools that engage in ongoing assessment of their initiatives seeking feedback from students, families, and community partners, can better understand the impact of their efforts. This reflective practice allows schools to celebrate successes, learn from challenges, and make informed adjustments to their strategies.

Leverage Technology Wisely

Finally, international case studies demonstrate the potential of technology to support cultural brokerage, whether through digital learning platforms that offer culturally diverse content or social media channels that facilitate community engagement. However, the wise use of technology—mindful of access issues and the digital divide—is essential to ensure that digital tools enhance rather than hinder cultural understanding and inclusion.

Lessons from international case studies on cultural brokerage in education emphasize the power of cultural diversity as a strength, the need for cultural competence, the importance of open communication, the value of community partnerships, the centrality of empathy and relationships, the necessity of adaptability and reflection, and the careful use of technology. These insights provide a roadmap for schools worldwide to navigate cultural differences and foster environments where every student can thrive.

Impact of cultural, social, and economic contexts on partnership strategies

Cultural, social, and economic contexts profoundly impact partnership strategies, shaping how collaborations are formed, sustained, and evolved. These contexts provide the backdrop against which schools and communities navigate their relationships, influencing their partnerships' priorities, approaches, and outcomes. Understanding these influences is crucial for developing strategies that are not only effective but also respectful and responsive to the needs and values of all stakeholders involved.

Cultural Context

The cultural context encompasses the beliefs, values, traditions, and social norms of the communities involved in the partnership. It significantly affects how partnerships are perceived, the form they take, and the activities they undertake. For instance, in communities where collective action and communal responsibility are highly valued, partnerships might focus on broad community engagement initiatives, leveraging these cultural strengths to support educational goals. Conversely, in cultures that emphasize individual achievement, partnerships might prioritize personal development opportunities for students. Navigating cultural nuances requires sensitivity and adaptability, ensuring that partnership strategies are culturally congruent and supportive of the community's identity.

Social Context

Social context refers to the community's social dynamics, structures, and issues, including family structures, social cohesion, and prevalent social challenges. This context can significantly influence the focus areas of partnerships. For example, in communities facing social challenges such as high crime rates or social disintegration, partnerships may prioritize safety and social cohesion, involving initiatives that bring the community together and promote a safe learning environment. On the other hand, in communities with strong social networks and support systems, partnerships might leverage these networks for mentoring programs or parent involvement initiatives. Understanding the community's social fabric helps tailor partnership strategies that address educational needs and contribute to social well-being.

Economic Context

The community's economic conditions, including poverty levels, employment rates, and resource access, are critical in shaping partnership strategies. In economically disadvantaged areas, partnerships often focus on addressing basic needs alongside educational goals, such as providing meals, health services, or after-school care, recognizing that students' basic needs must be met before effective learning can occur. Partnerships in these contexts may also seek to address economic challenges directly through vocational training programs or partnerships with local businesses to provide work experience opportunities for students. In contrast, in more affluent communities, partnerships might have the resources to focus on enrichment activities, advanced technology integration, or global learning experiences. Tailoring partnership strategies to the economic realities of the community ensures that efforts are relevant and impactful, addressing both immediate and long-term needs.

The interplay between cultural, social, and economic contexts and partnership strategies underscores the importance of contextual understanding in developing effective collaborations. This requires deep engagement with the community, listening to its members, and understanding their perspectives. Through this involvement, the community's assets, strengths, and difficulties are identified, which may be used to further educational objectives.

Furthermore, this understanding fosters a sense of respect and mutual benefit, where partnerships are not seen as one-sided but as collaborative efforts that recognize and value the contributions of all partners. It also highlights the need for flexibility and adaptability in partnership strategies, allowing for adjustments as contexts evolve or new challenges and opportunities arise.

Communities' cultural, social, and economic contexts profoundly impact the formation and execution of partnership strategies. By acknowledging and responding to these contexts, schools and community organizations can develop partnerships that are respectful, relevant, and responsive to the needs and values of the communities they serve. These contextually informed strategies enhance the effectiveness of partnerships and contribute to building more robust, more cohesive communities that support the holistic development of their members.

Global challenges in education and community engagement and how they are addressed

Global challenges in education and community engagement are diverse and multifaceted, reflecting the complex realities of our rapidly changing world. These challenges range from addressing educational inequalities and embracing technological advancements to fostering social cohesion and ensuring sustainability. Addressing these issues requires innovative approaches, collaborative efforts, and a commitment to creating inclusive, adaptable, resilient educational and community systems. Here are a few of these worldwide issues and the approaches used to solve them.

Educational Inequality

Educational inequality, which shows up as differences in access to high-quality education because of socioeconomic class, geography, gender, and ethnicity, is one of the most prevalent problems. Initiatives like community schools, equitable financing structures, and scholarship programs try to address this by offering top-notch instruction to all children. Governments and international organizations are also attempting to put laws encouraging inclusive education, guaranteeing that underrepresented and disadvantaged groups get the assistance they require to thrive.

Technological Advancements

The rapid pace of technological advancement presents opportunities and challenges for education and community engagement. While digital tools can enhance learning and connectivity, they also raise issues of digital divide and cyber safety. Addressing these challenges involves investing in digital infrastructure and literacy programs, particularly in underserved communities, to ensure equitable access to technology. Additionally, educational programs increasingly incorporate digital citizenship to equip students with the skills to navigate the online world safely and responsibly.

Globalization and Cultural Integration

As our world becomes more interconnected, fostering cultural understanding and integration becomes crucial. Education and community engagement initiatives increasingly focus on global competencies, such as cross-cultural communication and global awareness, to prepare students for a diverse and interconnected world. Programs that promote cultural exchange, language learning, and international collaboration are critical strategies in addressing the challenges of globalization, helping to build more inclusive and cohesive societies.

Environmental Sustainability

Environmental sustainability is urgently needed to influence education and community engagement initiatives worldwide. Schools are integrating sustainability education into their curricula, encouraging students to engage with climate change, conservation, and sustainable living issues. Community partnerships focused on environmental projects, such as school gardens, recycling programs, and conservation efforts, are also becoming more common and fostering a sense of environmental stewardship among students and community members.

Social Cohesion and Civic Engagement

Amidst rising social fragmentation and polarization, promoting social cohesion and civic engagement is a growing challenge. Education systems are responding by emphasizing civic education, community service, and social-emotional learning to foster a sense of community, empathy, and shared responsibility. Engaging students in community projects, service learning, and democratic processes encourages active citizenship and contributes to building more cohesive and resilient communities.

Health and Well-being

The global mental health and well-being challenges are receiving increased attention in education and community engagement efforts. Schools are adopting holistic approaches to student well-being, incorporating mental health education, support services, and wellness programs into their offerings. Partnerships with health organizations and community groups provide additional resources and support, emphasizing the importance of a supportive community in promoting the health and well-being of all members.

Addressing these global challenges requires a collective effort transcending borders and sectors. Collaboration among governments, educational institutions, community organizations, and international bodies is essential for sharing resources, knowledge, and best practices. Additionally, adopting a flexible and adaptive approach allows educational and community initiatives to evolve in response to emerging challenges and opportunities.

The global challenges facing education and community engagement are complex and interrelated, requiring innovative, collaborative, and inclusive responses. By addressing these challenges head-on, we can work towards a future where education empowers all individuals to reach their full potential and communities are strengthened by their members' active engagement and contribution.

CHAPTER 12

PREPARING FOR THE FUTURE: INNOVATIONS AND POLICY IMPLICATIONS

Anticipating changes in education and community dynamics is crucial in an ever-evolving world where technological advancements, societal shifts, and environmental challenges continually reshape the landscapes in which we live and learn. As we look toward the future, several key trends will likely influence the direction of education and the fabric of community life, requiring adaptability, foresight, and innovative thinking from educators, community leaders, and policymakers.

Increased Integration of Technology

The role of technology in education is expected to expand significantly, moving beyond supplementary tools to become central to the learning experience. This shift will result in more customized learning experiences tailored to each student's needs, preferences, and learning styles, thanks to the application of artificial intelligence and adaptive learning technologies. Additionally, virtual and augmented reality technologies are set to provide immersive learning experiences, making complex subjects more accessible and engaging. As technology becomes more integrated into education, communities must address the digital divide, ensuring equitable access to digital resources for all members.

Focus on Global Competencies

As the world becomes more interconnected, education systems will emphasize developing global competencies among students. This includes fostering cross-cultural understanding, environmental stewardship, and digital literacy, preparing students to navigate and contribute to a globalized world. Global concerns will be the focus of community involvement programs more and more, inspiring students to get involved in efforts that tackle issues like social justice, sustainability, and climate change.

Holistic Approaches to Student Well-being

Recognizing the critical link between well-being and learning, education systems will likely adopt more holistic approaches to student development. This includes academic skills, social-emotional learning, mental health support, and physical well-being. Community dynamics will shift to support these holistic approaches, with schools, families, and community organizations collaborating more closely to provide a supportive ecosystem for all students.

Emphasis on Lifelong Learning

As the pace of change accelerates, the importance of lifelong learning will become increasingly recognized. Education will not be seen as a phase that ends with formal schooling but as a continuous process that spans an individual's life. Community programs and partnerships will play a key role in facilitating lifelong learning opportunities, offering workshops, courses, and learning experiences that cater to all ages and stages of life.

Greater Community Involvement in Education

The future will likely see a blurring of the lines between schools and the wider community, with increased community involvement in education. Schools will become community hubs, hosting events, projects, and services that benefit students and community members. This shift will require communities to engage more in supporting education through volunteering, partnerships, or resource sharing.

Adaptation to Environmental Challenges

Environmental sustainability will become a more pressing concern, influencing education content and community initiatives. Schools will integrate sustainability education across the curriculum, while community projects will address local environmental challenges. This will involve teaching sustainability and modeling sustainable practices within schools and communities.

Inclusive and Equitable Education

Efforts to ensure inclusive and equitable education will intensify, focusing on removing barriers to access and success for all students, regardless of their background. This will involve addressing systemic inequalities, providing targeted support for marginalized groups, and ensuring that education systems reflect and value the diversity of the communities they serve.

Anticipating these changes requires a proactive approach, with educators, community leaders, and policymakers working together to envision the future of education and community life. By remaining aware of new trends and problems and being open to innovation and adaptation, we can ensure that educational institutions and community dynamics change in ways that fulfill the needs of all members and educate kids to flourish in an unpredictable but exciting future.

Innovative practices for the next generation of school-community partnerships

As we look toward the future, the next generation of school-community partnerships stands on the brink of a transformative era. Innovative practices will be vital in navigating this landscape, ensuring that these collaborations support educational outcomes and foster vibrant, resilient communities. Here are several forward-thinking strategies that promise to redefine the contours of school-community partnerships.

Leveraging Digital Platforms for Community Engagement

Digital platforms offer unparalleled opportunities for expanding the reach and depth of school-community partnerships. Beyond facilitating communication, these platforms can host virtual town halls, showcase student projects to a broader audience, and provide spaces for community members to offer feedback and ideas. Schools can collaborate with local tech companies to create custom platforms that serve as digital community hubs where resources, opportunities, and successes are shared.

Implementing Co-Learning Spaces

Imagine schools and community centers that double as co-learning spaces where students, parents, educators, and community members learn from each other. These spaces could host workshops on everything from coding and gardening to financial literacy and creative arts, led by community experts or passionate educators. This practice not only enriches the educational experience but also strengthens community ties by valuing the knowledge and skills present within the community.

Developing Community Problem-Solving Projects

School-community partnerships can tackle local issues through joint problem-solving projects. For instance, students could work alongside community organizations to develop sustainable solutions to environmental challenges, design apps to address local needs or initiate social campaigns. These projects encourage students to apply their learning in real-world contexts, fostering a sense of agency and civic responsibility while benefiting the community.

Fostering Cultural Exchange Programs

In an increasingly globalized world, cultural exchange programs within school-community partnerships can be crucial in promoting understanding and respect. These programs involve exchange visits, cultural festivals, and storytelling sessions that celebrate the diverse backgrounds of students and community members. Such initiatives enrich the curriculum and build a more inclusive community environment.

Creating Partnership Incubators

Partnership incubators can be a breeding ground for innovative collaboration between schools and community organizations. These incubators would support pilot projects, providing resources, mentorship, and evaluation to scale effective practices. By focusing on innovation and adaptability, partnership incubators can continuously evolve to meet changing educational and community needs.

Integrating Service Learning Throughout the Curriculum

Service learning, where educational goals are met through community service, can be integrated more deeply into the curriculum. This method helps the community and improves student learning. Projects can be designed to align with specific learning objectives across subjects, ensuring that service learning is a core component of the educational experience rather than an add-on.

Utilizing Data for Collaborative Decision-Making

Data-driven decision-making can significantly enhance the impact of school-community partnerships. By jointly collecting and analyzing data on student outcomes, community needs, and program effectiveness, schools and community partners can make informed decisions about where to focus their efforts. This practice ensures that partnerships are responsive to the needs of students and the community, maximizing their positive impact.

Prioritizing Sustainability in Partnerships

Environmental and programmatic sustainability should be a key consideration in the next generation of school-community partnerships. Initiatives that promote environmental stewardship can be integrated into partner hip activities, while the long-term sustainability of programs can be ensured through strategic planning, resource sharing, and community investment. This long-term view helps ensure that partnerships continue to benefit future generations.

Building Networks of School-Community Partnerships

Finally, creating networks of school-community partnerships can amplify their collective impact. These networks can facilitate sharing resources, ideas, and best practices while advocating for policies that support collaborative educational and community development efforts. By working together, partnerships can achieve more than they could individually, addressing systemic challenges and fostering widespread change.

The next generation of school-community partnerships promises a more connected, innovative, and resilient approach to education and community engagement. By embracing these innovative practices, schools, and communities can work together to create environments where every student thrives, and every community flourishes.

Policy recommendations for supporting cultural brokerage and partnership development

Supporting cultural brokerage and partnership development within educational contexts is crucial for creating inclusive and effective learning environments that reflect and respect the diversity of student populations. Policymakers play a vital role in fostering these initiatives through strategic planning and resource allocation. Several policy recommendations are designed to enhance cultural brokerage and strengthen school-community partnerships.

1. Allocate Funding for Cultural Competence Training

Ensure schools have the funds to provide ongoing cultural competence training for all educators and staff. This training should cover understanding cultural differences, effective communication strategies, and techniques for creating inclusive classroom environments. Funding could also support hiring specialists who can lead these training sessions and provide ongoing support to educators.

2. Establish Cultural Brokerage Roles

Encourage schools to establish dedicated roles for cultural brokers—individuals skilled in navigating between cultures and facilitating understanding and collaboration among students, families, and educators. Policymakers can support this by providing guidelines for the roles and responsibilities of cultural brokers and funding for their positions.

3. Promote Community Engagement Initiatives

Develop policies that encourage and reward schools for engaging with their local communities. This could include school grants establishing partnerships with local organizations, businesses, and cultural institutions and recognition programs highlighting successful community engagement initiatives.

4. Facilitate Access to Multilingual Resources

Ensure schools can access educational materials and resources in multiple languages to support learners from diverse linguistic backgrounds. Policies could mandate the provision of multilingual textbooks, digital resources, and translation services to facilitate communication between schools and non-English-speaking families.

5. Support the Integration of Cultural Content in Curricula

Recommend that educational curricula include content that reflects the cultural diversity of the student population. This could involve developing guidelines for incorporating cultural studies, histories, and languages into the standard curriculum and supporting the creation of specialized courses focusing on local cultural heritage.

6. Foster Digital Platforms for School-Community Collaboration

Encourage developing and using digital platforms that facilitate collaboration and communication between schools and communities. Policymakers could support this through funding for technology infrastructure and training for educators and community members on using these platforms effectively.

7. Implement Policies for Equitable Partnership Development

Create policies that ensure equitable access to partnership opportunities for all schools, especially those in under-resourced or marginalized communities. This could include targeted funding, support for capacity building, and incentives for organizations to partner with schools in these areas.

8. Encourage Research and Evaluation

Promote research and evaluation of cultural brokerage and school-community partnership initiatives to identify best practices and areas for improvement. Policies could support partnerships with universities and research institutions to conduct studies and disseminate findings to the broader educational community.

9. Create Advisory Bodies for Cultural Brokerage and Partnerships

Establish advisory bodies at the local or regional level that include educators, community leaders, cultural experts, and policymakers. These bodies can guide the implementation of cultural brokerage and partner IP initiatives, share resources and best practices, and advocate for supportive policies and funding.

By implementing these policy recommendations, governments and educational authorities can create a supportive framework that enables schools to effectively engage in cultural brokerage and develop strong, meaningful partnerships with their communities. Such initiatives enrich students' educational experience and foster greater understanding, respect, and collaboration across diverse cultural landscapes.

Building resilient and adaptable partnership frameworks for future challenges

Building resilient and adaptable partnership frameworks is essential for effectively preparing schools and communities to face future challenges. As the world continues to change at an unprecedented pace, these frameworks must be designed to withstand pressures, adapt to new realities, and seize emerging opportunities. Here are critical strategies for developing such frameworks:

Emphasize Flexible-adaptability

Policy should prioritize the creation of partnership frameworks that are inherently flexible and adaptable. This means encouraging partnerships to adopt a growth mindset and be willing to evolve their objectives, strategies, and activities in response to changing circumstances. Policies could encourage regular review and revision of partnership agreements and plans, ensuring they remain relevant and responsive to current needs and opportunities.

Foster a Culture of Continuous Learning

Policies should support a culture of continuous learning within partnerships, emphasizing the importance of ongoing professional development, shared learning experiences, and cross-sector exchanges. By investing in the development of all individuals involved—from educators and community leaders to policymakers and students—partnerships can enhance their collective ability to navigate future challenges.

Encourage Innovation and Experimentation

Establishing an atmosphere that promotes experimentation and creativity is essential. Policies that encourage this include using grants or incentives for partnerships that pilot new approaches to collaboration, community engagement, or educational programming. Embracing a trial-and-error approach, where failures are viewed as learning opportunities, can lead to breakthrough solutions and strengthen the partnership's resilience.

Strengthen Communication Channels

Effective communication is the backbone of any resilient partnership. Policies should facilitate the development of robust communication channels that ensure a transparent, open, and timely exchange of information among all stakeholders. This includes leveraging digital tools to enhance connectivity and accessibility and ensuring that communication strategies are inclusive and reach all community members.

Promote Equity and Inclusivity

Resilient partnerships prioritize equity and inclusivity, ensuring all voices are heard and valued. Policies should target historically marginalized or underrepresented groups and require the participation of different viewpoints in the design and execution of partnership activities. This approach enriches the partnership and strengthens its foundation by building trust and mutual respect.

Build on Community Strengths and Assets

Recognizing and building upon communities' strengths and assets can enhance the resilience of partnership frameworks. Policies should encourage asset-based community development approaches, leveraging existing resources, talents, and capacities within the community. This empowers communities and creates a more sustainable basis for partnership activities.

Prepare for Crisis and Change

Given the inevitability of crises and change, partnership frameworks must include emergency preparedness and crisis management strategies. Policies could support the development of contingency plans, emergency funds, and rapid response teams within partnerships. Partners can respond more effectively by preparing for potential challenges and continuing their essential work even in difficult times.

Support Collaborative Governance Structures

Finally, resilient partnership frameworks benefit from collaborative governance structures involving all stakeholder groups' representatives. Policies should encourage the creation of joint decision-making bodies, advisory committees, and feedback mechanisms that facilitate shared governance. This collaborative approach ensures that decision-making is inclusive, transparent, and accountable.

Building resilient and adaptable partnership frameworks requires a multifaceted approach emphasizing flexibility, continuous learning, innovation, effective communication, equity, community strengths, preparedness for change, and collaborative governance. By implementing policies that support these principles, schools, and communities can develop partnerships capable of navigating future challenges and thriving in the face of them, ultimately leading to more robust, more vibrant educational environments and communities.

Throughout our exploration of strengthening school-community partnerships and the pivotal role of cultural brokers, several key insights and lessons have emerged that are instrumental in guiding future endeavors in these areas. First and foremost, acknowledging cultural diversity as a significant asset within educational environments underscores the importance of embracing and integrating these varied cultural perspectives directly into the fabric of educational strategies and community engagements.

A crucial lesson learned is the indispensable value of cultural competence among educators and administrators. Cultivating an environment that acknowledges and actively celebrates cultural diversity requires a deep understanding and appreciation of these differences. This competence becomes the cornerstone upon which practical and meaningful engagement with communities, particularly those with diverse or marginalized populations, is built.

The exploration also highlighted the nuanced challenges schools and communities face in fostering effective partnerships. These include navigating linguistic barriers, ensuring equitable access to technological resources, and overcoming socio-economic disparities. Addressing these challenges requires innovative, flexible strategies adaptable to each community's needs and circumstances.

The role of technology emerged as a double-edged sword. While it offers remarkable opportunities for enhancing communication and educational outcomes, it also presents challenges related to digital access and literacy. Ensuring that technological interventions are accessible and inclusive for all community members is paramount for leveraging these tools effectively.

Another significant insight is the critical function of cultural brokers in bridging the gaps between schools and diverse communities. These individuals, whether educators, community leaders, or external specialists, play a crucial role in facilitating understanding, communication, and cooperation across cultural divides. Their work is instrumental in ensuring that engagement strategies are effective, respectful of cultural nuances, and inclusive of all voices.

Finally, the exploration reaffirmed the importance of continuous learning, adaptation, and collaboration among all education and community development stakeholders. Building and sustaining successful school-community partnerships requires a commitment to ongoing evaluation and feedback and the willingness to innovate and adapt strategies in response to emerging challenges and opportunities.

These insights and lessons form a solid foundation for future efforts to enhance education quality through robust school-community partnerships and effective cultural brokerage. They highlight the need for a concerted, collaborative approach that prioritizes inclusivity, equity, and cultural competence in all educational and community engagement aspects.

To elevate the future of education and community well-being, a unified call to action is imperative for strengthening school-community partnerships. Educators, administrators, community leaders, and policymakers must prioritize and invest in building relationships rooted in mutual respect, shared goals, and a commitment to inclusivity. This involves embracing community diversity as a valuable asset and actively seeking to understand and integrate varied cultural perspectives into educational strategies.

A strategic emphasis on professional development in cultural competence is crucial for all involved in education. Schools should foster environments where every family feels seen, heard, and valued, recognizing that successful engagement is predicated on respect for cultural nuances and effective communication. Additionally, leveraging technology to enhance accessibility and learning while ensuring that these digital tools are equitable and inclusive is essential.

Collaboration is key. By forging strong connections with local organizations, businesses, and cultural institutions, schools can create a vibrant ecosystem of support for students. Flexibility, creativity, and a readiness to adjust to the changing demands of communities are necessary for this team effort. Let's commit to these principles, ensuring every child has the support, resources, and community backing to succeed academically and beyond.

Cultural brokers' role in fostering collaboration between schools and communities is critical in the tapestry of educational success and community engagement. By bridging cultural divides, these individuals enhance understanding and communication and embody the spirit of inclusivity and mutual respect that is foundational to strong partnerships. Cultural brokers navigate the complexities of diverse backgrounds with empathy and insight, making them indispensable in creating environments where every student can thrive.

Their work goes beyond mere language translation or mediation of cultural misunderstandings; it involves building trust, respect, and genuine relationships between educators, students, and families. By valuing and integrating the rich cultural assets that diverse communities bring, cultural brokers help create educational experiences that reflect and are responsive to all students' needs.

Cultural brokers catalyze change, driving schools and communities toward more equitable and effective collaboration. Their role underscores the importance of cultural competence and highlights the power of understanding and respecting diversity in achieving educational equity. As we look to the future of education, the contributions of cultural brokers in fostering collaboration and enhancing school-community partnerships will undoubtedly remain paramount.

As we conclude this exploration into the vibrant world of school-community partnerships and the invaluable role of cultural brokers within these frameworks, it's essential to acknowledge the collective efforts that make such collaborations possible. The journey through understanding the complexities, challenges, and innovations in building solid and inclusive partnerships has underscored the importance of unity, respect, and shared vision.

Special thanks are due to the educators, administrators, community leaders, and cultural brokers whose dedication and hard work lie at the heart of these transformative partnerships. Their unwavering commitment to fostering environments where every student can succeed, irrespective of their cultural or linguistic background, is truly inspiring. Acknowledgment must also be extended to the researchers and policymakers who provide the insights and frameworks necessary for these partnerships to flourish.

The families and communities that actively engage with schools deserve recognition for their vital role in enriching the educational experience. Their contributions ensure that education remains a communal endeavor rooted in the collective aspiration for a brighter, more inclusive future.

Moving forward, let us carry the lessons learned and insights gained with a sense of purpose and optimism. The journey toward more robust, more resilient school-community partnerships is ongoing, and it is through continued collaboration, innovation, and respect for diversity that we will navigate the challenges ahead.

In closing, this exploration is a step in the ongoing dialogue about the power of partnership and collaboration in education. May it inspire further engagement, research, and action, driving us toward a future where every child benefits from the strength of their community and every community thrives on the success of its children. Here's to the next chapter of collaboration, understanding, and growth.

References

Epstein, J. L., Sanders, M. G., Simon, B. S., Salinas, K. C., Jansorn, N. R., & Van Voorhis, F. L. (2019). *School, Family, and Community Partnerships: Your Handbook for Action* (4th ed.). Corwin Press.

Harris, O. (2019). *A phenomenological study of Epstein's parental involvement framework with middle-school English language learner (ELL) teachers and language specialists*. Concordia University.

www.ingramcontent.com/pod-product-compliance
Lightning Source LLC
Chambersburg PA
CBHW051236130726
47988CB00001B/370